The Salmon Mysteries Workbook

This workbook belongs to:

_____

Reimagining began on this date:

_____

Also by Kim Antieau

Novels
The Blue Tail
Broken Moon
Butch
Church of the Old Mermaids
Coyote Cowgirl
Deathmark
The Desert Siren
The Fish Wife
Her Frozen Wild
The Gaia Websters
Jewelweed Station
The Jigsaw Woman
Maternal Instincts
Mercy, Unbound
The Monster's Daughter
Queendom: Feast of the Saints
The Rift
Ruby's Imagine
Swans in Winter
Whackadoodle Times
Whackadoodle Times Two

Nonfiction
Answering the Creative Call
Certified: Learning to Repair Myself and the World in the Emerald City
Counting on Wildflowers: An Entanglement
Old Mermaids Book of Days and Nights
Under the Tucson Moon

Collections
Entangled Realities (with Mario Milosevic)
The First Book of Old Mermaids Tales
Tales Fabulous and Fairy
Trudging to Eden

Chapbook
Blossoms

Blog
www.kimantieau.com

The Salmon Mysteries Workbook

Reimagining the Eleusinian Mysteries

Kim Antieau

Green Snake
PUBLISHING

The Salmon Mysteries Workbook:
Reimagining the Eleusinian Mysteries
by Kim Antieau

© 2001, 2010, 2017 by Kim Antieau
All rights reserved.

ISBN: 978-1-949644-26-5

No part of this book may be reproduced without written permission of the author.

Designed by Mario Milosevic.
Cover image copyright © Joanna Powell Colbert.
Special thanks to Lucia Ploskey.

www.kimantieau.com

Green Snake Publishing
www.greensnakepublishing.com

*In memory of
Marija Gimbutas and Patricia Monaghan:
We will not forget.*

*With love and gratitude to
Vicki Noble and Demetra George*

*Special thanks to Ruth Ford Biersdorf for her incredible
attention to detail and her kindness and generosity.*

*With hope for Peace,
I send* The Salmon Mysteries Workbook *out into the world.
May the Nch'I-Wana soon run red with wild salmon again.*

Contents

Introduction to the Workbook
9

Preface to The Salmon Mysteries
11

A Word About Words and Other Things
17

Introduction to The Mystai Guidebook
23

The Salmon Mysteries: A Reimagining of the Demeter and Persephone Myth
33

A Little Herstory, or How to Become Mythwise
45

What Happened in Eleusis?
49

How Should You Prepare?
55

Day One: Day of Commitment
61

Day Two: Day of Gathering
67

Day Three: Day of Purification
73

Day Four: Day of Coyote
81

Day Five: Day of Snake
89

Day Six: Procession Day
95

Day Seven: Day of the Bear
99

Day Eight: *Mysteriotides Nychtes*, Night of the Mysteries
105

Day of Mystery
113

Day Nine: Day of the Salmon
123

Song of the Salmon
131

Notes
137

Bibliography
141

Introduction to the Workbook

Here it is at long last: *The Salmon Mysteries Workbook*. I created it in the hopes that it would give you the space to play, to create art, to write, to be full of your true self while participating in The Salmon Mysteries.

The Salmon Mysteries: A Guidebook to a Reimagining of the Eleusinian Mysteries has been a part of my life for almost two decades. I had envisioned The Salmon Mysteries becoming a community event every year. This hasn't happened yet. So far, people have been doing the mysteries on their own or with a friend or two. That's fine! As long as someone is celebrating the Mysteries somewhere then it is making a difference in the world. When we celebrate the wheel of the year, the seasons of the year, when we connect more fully with Nature and our own sweet selves, it is all for the better. We then feel more connected to our environment, we're more in sync with the ecology of the place that keeps us alive, and then we are more willing to protect it, to keep the air, water, and land safe and clean, healthy and vibrant.

We mostly placed the journal prompts before the blank space where you can draw, paint, or collage, not because you should necessarily journal first—in fact some of the journal prompts are about your experience doing art—but because we thought it worked better for the layout of the workbook.

We left a space for you to record dreams. But don't worry if you don't have any. When I'm in the midst of a process like this, I often don't remember my dreams at all. You can practice what Robert Moss calls "sidewalk tarot" and others call dreaming in waking life. Look for signs—for the unusual—as you go about your day. For instance, one day a huge tom cat appeared on my front lawn, cleaning his fur. He reminded me of a panther. I figured I was getting some kind of magic from him. Another time, I found a small tree branch on the sidewalk—far from any trees—and it was in the shape of the Algiz rune. For me, the Algiz rune is all about strength and protection. I was glad to find it because I felt like I needed it! Things like that. Note them and write them in your workbook. You might want to explore them further with a journey or meditation.

I encourage you to make this workbook your art piece each year. It contains the complete text from the original book (with some tweaks and changes) as well as new material. I've put in journal prompts for you, but this is yours. Do with it what you will. It's not a class. I'm not going to be grading you. No one is. Have a ball with it.

Preface to The Salmon Mysteries

She is the mother of all, for contained in her are the seeds of all.
—Hildegard of Bingen, translated by Gabriele Uhlein

The body cannot be whole alone. Persons cannot be whole alone.... To try and heal the body alone is to collaborate in the destruction of the body. Healing is impossible in loneliness.
—Wendell Berry, *The Unsettling of America*

Welcome to the Mysteries! The Eleusinian Mysteries have fascinated me for years. After all, what happened on the last two nights of this nine-day celebration and worship of the goddesses Demeter and Persephone had been kept secret for over 3,000 years despite the participation of thousands of people. The more I studied the Mysteries, however, the less I was interested in solving a mystery. Instead I wondered what it would have been like to worship a goddess all of my life: to think of the Divine as female. To see representations of Her everywhere, artwork where someone with a body *like mine* was Goddess. It gave me chills.

I believe we may be hardwired for cyclical activity—for routine, ceremonies, celebrations. My fondest memories of childhood are of Halloween, Christmas, and Easter. Most of the actual celebrations blur into one mysterious Halloween, one mystical Christmas, and one colorful Easter; each year is not distinguishable from the other, but the act of celebrating in a similar manner on each holiday became touchstones of stability in the ever-changing life of a child.

I was raised Catholic but left that religion long ago because its rituals and doctrines were meaningless to me. The lack of respect for and exclusion of women in every organized religion I studied kept me far from any thought of the Divine until I rediscovered what I had known as a child and forgotten as an adult: the Divine is in Nature. Nature is always present, always producing air for me to breathe, water I can drink, and food I can eat. She is the ultimate Mother. When I learned that our ancestors had most likely worshipped the Earth as Goddess and lived in relative peace and harmony with Her and one another, my entire worldview changed.

I realized *we didn't have to be killers*. Those who said humans were biologically predetermined to kill each other and destroy the environment didn't know the truth; life did not have to be about death, dying, and killing. Death was only part of a lifelong cycle. Men killing people for eternity (and it was usually men doing the killing) was not the only reality or the only story.

We needed a new story.

We needed a new way of seeing the world, of being in the world.

We needed a new cycle—one that was not permeated with violence.

At the core of the Demeter and Persephone myth, underneath the parts added by patriarchal storytellers that I stripped away like layers of ugly old paint, is a story of love, cyclical change, and rebirth: a story for our times.

Although I set The Salmon Mysteries here in the Pacific Northwest and it deals with the wild salmon and their slide toward extinction, The Salmon Mysteries could take place anywhere. Just as The Eleusinian Mysteries were most likely adapted from Cretan ceremonies to fit into Greek society, so The Salmon Mysteries can be adapted to wherever you make your home. You may not live alongside a Big River, but a river (or another body of water) figures into your ecological life, whether you are aware of it or not.

Waterways all over our country—and the world—are in great peril. The sacred salmon is extinct in many places already. But the salmon could just as well be the sacred owl, redwood, jaguar, bear, ladyslipper, or hummingbird; they are by their very *Nature* sacred, holy. The word holy comes from *kailo* which means 'whole, hale, uninjured, health.' The existence (or extinction) of the salmon, owl, jaguar and other species indicates whether our environment is whole, healthy, hale.

I see The Salmon Mysteries as a way of life and an annual celebration, something which will bring positive change in the world and become a touchstone of joy and stability in our lives. Adapt it to your own community and to whatever time of year seems appropriate. Make it meaningful to you.

Mystai Tasks

Where does your drinking water come from? What did that last water report say about the chemicals in your water?

Draw and/or paint and color your favorite waterway here or on a separate sheet of paper.

How did it feel drawing your waterway? How does it feel to be with this water? What does it say to you? Visit it, if you can, after you've drawn it and written about it. Sit with it. Meditate with it. Really experience it sensually rather than intellectually. How is the experience different and the same as before?

A Word about Words and Other Things

The fields belong to woman.... The mystery astounds her.
And she is the mystery, the fields belong to woman.
—Betty De Shong Meador

A *mystes* was an initiate into the Mysteries. In the Eleusinian Mysteries, the *mystai* began their preparation six months earlier during the Lesser Eleusinian Mysteries. Mystai is the plural of mystes, and it is pronounced mis-tie (rhymes with sty).

Melissa was a title given to someone who was a priestess, most often a priestess to Artemis or Demeter. Melissa means priestess and bee, and Demeter was called the pure mother bee.

Many goddesses were linked with bees and honey. Honey was used as a preservative, healing agent, and burial encasing, and the ancients saw honey as having magical life-giving qualities. Matrifocal cultures often buried their dead in "round 'bee-hive' tombs."[1] Honey could be brewed into an intoxicant, and the Melissae probably used this drink in their ecstatic rituals.

According to Norma Lorre Goodrich, a Melissa was an Asian Priestess[2] (another clue to Demeter's origins which I will discuss later). Scholar Mara Lynn Keller wonders if these priestesses "saw their role as helping bring forth the fruitfulness of the Earth Mother, drawing from her the sweet sustenance of their living."[3] Melissae is the plural of Melissa, and it's pronounced me-lis-see (rhymes with key).

Someone who is experiencing the Mysteries for the first time is a Mystes, part of the Mystai; she is an initiate. Once a woman has completed the Mysteries, she is then one of the Melissae, now a priestess of Demeter, no longer an initiate. Each year you experience the Mysteries, you can come to them as a Mystes—an initiate once again—or you may act as Priestess/Melissa for that year. It is your choice.

Remember, no one can truly initiate you. No hierarchy. No priest or priestess. When I call someone a priestess, I am using the term as a rotating title of honor or authority for that moment. Next ceremony, someone else is priestess—someone else acts as a teacher or facilitator for a time until the student or initiate is ready to become the teacher. Imagining the face of the Divine as female doesn't mean we just change the genitals of the god and keep in place all the meaningless rituals and oppressive hierarchy. This is a new way. A truly Sacred Way. You dance your own dance.

Mystai Tasks

Draw yourself first as initiate and then as priestess or priest here or on a separate sheet. You can draw each side by side or use the extra space to give each their own page. Give yourself great powers, beautiful clothes, yummy food, sparkling gems: whatever will feel good to you. You don't have to be realistic, you don't have to be a great artist. Draw a stick figure if that's what you can do! What is the difference between you as an initiate and then you as a priestess? Then journal about how it felt to draw yourself as both. Have fun with it. (There are blank pages to draw on at the end of the chapter.)

_____

_____

_____

_____

_____

_____

Record dreams here.

20 Kim Antieau

Introduction to The Mystai Guidebook

Let the mystery be.
—Iris DeMent

What was it like to grow up in a culture where the divine was considered female? What was it like to gaze at signs of life—the goddess, creativity, and fertility—when you worshipped? What was it like to share this incredible experience of the Goddess with your entire community? *Did it reverberate through your whole divine body, shaking joy and love and faith into every cell, into your soul?*

I believe it did.

I have long wanted to bring the Eleusinian Mysteries to our continent and tailor this ancient inspiring celebration to the Natural cycles of the Pacific Northwest and the Columbia River Gorge in particular. The Eleusinian Mysteries, an annual nine-day event celebrated in Greece for nearly 2,000 years, probably began somewhere in the middle of the second millennium B.C.E.[4] Many scholars believe the Mysteries originally came from Crete, where archaeological and historical evidence suggests a peaceful egalitarian society thrived. The goddess was worshipped, the Mysteries were not secret, and the abduction and rape of Persephone were not part of the myth.[5] Once in Greece, the abduction of Persephone was added and the rites of the last two nights of the Mysteries became secret. Of the thousands of people who participated in these rituals, no one ever told what happened, at least not in print or in any surviving artistic renderings.

In the basic myth of the Nature Goddess Demeter and Her Daughter Persephone, Persephone decides to travel to the Underworld (or is abducted by the King of the Underworld). Demeter is bereft. She wanders the countryside looking for Her Daughter, in grief and despair. She is Earth Mother; without her attention, the countryside withers. She stops at Eleusis, disguised, and works as a nursemaid. In an attempt to relieve Demeter's suffering and make the grieving goddess smile, Baubo lifts her skirts and reveals her vulva to Demeter. Demeter laughs. Soon after, Persephone returns to her mother as a mature woman; because she has eaten food in the Underworld she must return to the Underworld for part of each year, or she willingly returns every year to help the Dead, depending upon the version of the tale. This story is a seasonal metaphor, blood mystery reenactment, and tale of transformation. It is about overcoming great sorrow and grief to live in the world again.

According to Mara Lynn Keller, the rites of Demeter and Persephone "speak to the experiences of life that remain through all times the most mysterious—birth, sexuality, death—and also to the greatest mystery of all, enduring love. In these ceremonies, women and men expressed joy in the beauty and abundance of nature...and in the rebirth of the human spirit, even through suffering and death."[6] The Roman Cicero wrote that because of the Eleusinian Mysteries, "We have been given a reason not only to live in joy, but also to die with better hope."[7] After studying archaeological data from that period, Keller concluded that the Mysteries of Demeter and Persephone were "essentially mysteries of love. Their main purpose was to bring an experience of love to the most important life passages."[8]

Although the tale of Demeter and Her Daughter can be called an agricultural myth, especially since Demeter is later equated with Ceres, the cereal (grain) goddess, it is also a story of the cycles of life in a particular place. In Eleusis, agriculture was preeminent. Where I live in the Columbia River Gorge, the most profound and mysterious cycle we witness yearly is the cycle of the salmon. I believe the salmon are the soul of the Pacific Northwest. I am not alone in this belief. The salmon are central to the religious and daily life of many Native People in the Pacific Rim.

The Ainu, who presently live in Japan, most likely came from coastal Siberia. In the Ainu cosmology, the world was made up of humans (*ainu*) and the divine (*kamuy*). The *kamuy* were not all-powerful god figures from heaven but were—literally—the Natural world, and "the first salmon who came up the river each year were regarded as the sacred messengers of the *kamuy* and were treated with respect."[9]

For the Native People who lived along the Columbia River, fishing for salmon was a way of life. "Salmon were a gift from the Creator and sacred," writes Elizabeth Woody.[10] Not far from where I live is a place that used to be Celilo Falls, the Great Falls. Area Natives called it *Wyam*, which means "Echo of Falling Water" or "Sound of Water upon the Rocks."[11] Archaeological evidence indicates that this site was used by humans for at least 12,000 years. Water roared over basalt cliffs and rapids, creating three main fishing sites. Native People built wooden platforms out over the Nch'I-Wana (Columbia River). They stood on these wooden platforms or on rocks—a rope around their waists to keep them from falling into the water—and caught fish using lines, nets, and harpoons. Women prepared the fish once it was caught. Children played nearby.

Then the Corps of Engineers built a dam. On March 10, 1957, the dam was put into service. The water slowly rose. The People stood on both sides of the Nch'I-Wana watching, until the water drowned the Falls. The Great Falls fell silent, the voice of the Mother was stilled. The lullaby the People had heard all of their lives was gone, the song their ancestors had listened to for millennia silenced.

Their grief was so awesome that the People turned their backs on the Big River as the Great Falls gurgled into silence. Their grief continues to this day. If you drive by the place now, you would have no idea that a waterfall once broke the River into dangerous rapids. There is only quiet: except for the sound of the wind and passing automobiles. Some believe losing Celilo Falls was the worst thing that ever happened to this area. The wild salmon runs have gotten smaller and smaller each year since then.

Elizabeth Woody says her people do not talk about the dam and Celilo much. "The grief is so great," she writes. "Today we know Celilo Falls as more than a lost landmark. It was a place as revered as one's own mother."[12]

Salmon have been important to many peoples, including my own Irish and French ancestors. The Celts believed the sacred salmon were the wisest of creatures as well as one of the oldest. They came from the Well of Wisdom where they were imbued with divine illumination, in part from eating the hazelnuts that dropped into the Well.[13] Poets longed to eat the sacred salmon so that they too would know all.

Many Native tribes from the Pacific Northwest performed particular ceremonies to insure the return of the salmon.[14] Likewise, the Greeks considered the Eleusinian Mysteries necessary to sustain life as they knew it. When a Catholic Emperor in 364 C.E. forbade the people to worship any gods but the Christian god, Praetextatus—a religious and political official who was not Greek but who had been initiated into the Eleusinian Mysteries—begged the Emperor to change his mind, declaring that life would be unlivable unless the Greeks were allowed to observe the Sacred Mysteries properly.[15]

Throughout history—and herstory—people have celebrated the cycles of life. Many believed these meaningful celebrations were a part of the fabric of existence. If a community stopped performing these rituals, it was as if they were deliberately pulling the thread on a blanket, only this blanket was the blanket of life, the tapestry of life, as it were. Soon, nothing would be left of the blanket—or life—except a pile of threads, colorful maybe, but without heart, soul, and meaning. Chaos.

Were our ancestors right? Could ceremony help save the world? Can ritual save the salmon? Can it save us? Aboriginal Peoples around the planet were prevented from practicing their religions by various invaders over the millennia. Maybe the First People were wise in ways the invaders did not understand. Perhaps the ecological destruction of the biosphere is a result of humans forgetting our deep abiding connection to Nature; because we do not regularly celebrate and honor the forces of Nature, we lose that necessary connection that sustains all of life. Meaningful celebration, which is essentially what ceremony is, leads to understanding, love, and connection.

After many years of studying the Eleusinian Mysteries and the myth of Demeter and Her Daughter, I decided to reshape and rewrite—reimagine—the tale and incorporate into it the Natural cycles of the Pacific Northwest, embodying these cycles in the journey of the salmon. I have chosen to tell the story from a prepatriarchal viewpoint, without the abduction and rape of Persephone (following in such big footsteps as Charlene Spretnak, Starhawk, and Carolyn McVickar Edwards).

I also devised a nine-day celebration of the Mysteries which mirrors the ancient celebration and alters it so that it is meaningful to present-day life. When ceremony loses its meaning, when the celebrants no longer know why they are performing certain rites, the power of the rituals disappear.

Nine is a sacred number, the number of the Crone, the number of the Goddess times three, the number of days Demeter wandered looking for her daughter. The nine-day process of the Mysteries outlined in this guidebook is really a culmination of months, years, decades of your "being." You could just as easily work on one of these steps for an entire month—beginning on Solstice, December 21, for instance, and concluding nine months later with the Autumnal Equinox. Or you could begin the process at any time of year you felt was appropriate. You decide.

The Eleusinian Mysteries, and now The Salmon Mysteries, are about honoring the cycles in our own lives as well as the Natural cycles. Celebrating these

Mysteries helps us remember who we are so we can become who we want to be within these inevitable cycles. As we honor the cycles of the Salmon, we honor ourselves, and we hope to help restore some balance to the Natural processes.

This workbook can help you create ceremony and ritual that is unique to the land where you live. You can use it to initiate yourselves and others into the mysteries of Demeter and Persephone, into the mysteries of Eleusis—into the true mysteries of self-revelation: to know thyself. This is all about becoming full of your true self and helping you and others connect with yourself and each other.

I have celebrated these Mysteries alone. I have celebrated them with a group of women over nine days. I have honored the Mysteries in one day with a community celebration. Use this guidebook as a stepping off place to celebrate in your own way.

For each day of the Mysteries, I discuss what we know happened on that day in Greece. I then connect those events to The Salmon Mysteries. Finally, I suggest Mystai Tasks: something for you to do—alone or with others—on that particular day to prepare for the Mysteries.

I understand that many of you have extremely busy lives. What I lay out here may feel like too much to do over nine days. As I said before, adapt this to your own life. Remember, though, part of what we need to examine as we re-enchant ourselves and the world is our own compulsion for busy-ness.

Are you ready to begin?

Mystai Tasks

What plants, animals, and waterways are endangered where you live? Which are thriving? It's important to celebrate that which is thriving as well as protect that which is in danger. Do you have a favorite wild thing near where you live: plant, animal, waterway, or piece of land? Draw this "wild thing" on the blank pages at the end of the chapter in whatever way feels fun and sacred.

Write a poem or a song to honor this wild thing. What can you do to protect the land or the wild creatures? They are your neighbors, and you are theirs. What would a good neighbor do? It doesn't have to be huge. You don't have to decide to save the world. It can be as simple as picking up trash when you walk or hike. It can be as simple as joining your local Audubon chapter. You'll figure it out.

Record dreams here.

The Salmon Mysteries: A Reimagining of the Demeter and Persephone Myth

The universe is made of stories, not of atoms.
—Muriel Rukeyser

Every spring, Demeter and Her Daughter walked through fields of wildflowers. They picked this one and that one to eat as they went on their way. Demeter liked the cool sweetness of the chickweed; Her Daughter liked the tangy violet petals and leaves. From every step Demeter took, a wildflower sprang. Her Daughter laughed as the flowers bloomed; she leaned down to smell each one. At the rivers, creeks, and streams, Demeter and Her Daughter stopped to watch the golden salmon on their way out to the Nch'I-Wana—the Big River—then to the Ocean.

Demeter told Her Daughter the story of the salmon every spring when they celebrated the First Salmon and in the autumn when they celebrated the Salmon Homecoming: how they hatched from orange-red eggs buried safely in a sandy river bottom by their mother in a place where their mother's own parents had been born and their parents before them.

"After they hatch and grow, the beautiful salmon swim down Nch'I-Wana," Demeter said, "and their bodies change so that they can survive in the Ocean, where they live for many years until it is time to return home. Then nothing can stop them! They change once again as they travel from the Ocean to the river. They become red with the passion of creation, with the fire of determination. When they reach the spawning beds, they lay their eggs—or fertilize them if they are male—and then they die, and the nutrients of their bodies become the food for their children.

"Nch'I-Wana is Life, and Salmon is the soul of that Life—of our lives," Demeter said. "Salmon are like the blood running through our veins; they keep the Big River going, just as our blood keeps us going."

Every autumn, Demeter and Her Daughter walked through fields of berries. They picked this one and that one to drop into their baskets or pop into their mouths. Her Daughter especially liked the huckleberries, Demeter the salmonberries. At each river, creek, and stream, Demeter and Her Daughter stopped to watch the blood red salmon swim upstream, leaping up watery basalt cliffs and rocky creeks. Her Daughter was certain she had never seen anything as beautiful as the giant red salmon twisting in mid-air, trying with all its considerable might to make it up the river and back home again.

One spring while Demeter walked in one field with several companions, Her Daughter ran to Falling Creek to get a drink of water. The river bed was swollen with snowmelt and had flooded its banks with its new-found body, yet Her Daughter could still see the flashes of gold as salmon made their way downstream, like pieces of light lost by the sun. The gold matched the color of her dress. She glanced at the field where her mother danced, flowers growing from her footsteps. Demeter had always cautioned Her Daughter to be careful near the water. "The River is our life," Demeter said, "but it is easy to fall into her dreamy arms." Of course, her Mother was mostly speaking of Nch'I-Wana—the Big River—not this Falling Creek. Her Daughter looked back at the flashing water. What would it feel like to touch the fish as they traveled toward the Ocean? Would it feel like the sun? Would it feel like the Soul of the World?

She reached out to the water. Her feet slipped on the water's edge, and she lost her balance. She cried out as she tried to get her footing again, but it was too late. She fell into the water.

Demeter heard Her Daughter's cries and raced toward her instantly, turning in time to see her slip into the water without even making a splash. When Demeter reached the edge of the creek, She looked frantically for Her Daughter but saw only water and salmon. She waded into the turbulent water, ignoring the warnings from her companions. She was a powerful being, responsible for life on Earth: She could withstand the water from a creek! She peered into the water. Salmon knocked against her legs. She cried out for Her Daughter. No response.

"Crow!" Demeter shouted.

"I am here!" Crow responded.

"You are good at finding shiny things," She said. "Run along this river and see if you can find my daughter."

"I will do this," Crow said. And Crow flew away, following the bends of the creek.

Demeter stepped out of the water and ran along the banks of the river, watching and calling out for Her Daughter, riparian branches and saplings slapping her in the face as She ran, panic clutching her heart.

Finally She reached the shore of the Nch'I-Wana. She had seen no signs of Her Daughter, dead or alive. Crow flew down to her.

"I am sorry, Demeter," Crow said. "But I did not see your Daughter. Only salmon."

Demeter nodded. They both knew what that meant: either Her Daughter was dead or she was now one of the Salmon People. In any case, Persephone was lost to Demeter. She sank to the ground and wept.

"Why has this happened!" She wailed. "I have done all that I should! I have given to the people all of my gifts! It is not right that you take away my only pleasure, my heart's desire!"

No one answered her cries, although her companions tried to comfort her when they reached her side. She was inconsolable. She walked alongside Nch'I-Wana, crying and calling out for Her Daughter. The River People began an extensive search for Her Daughter. Day after day they looked. Day after day Demeter walked and walked, searching for Her Daughter.

Finally one of the Elders of the River People said, "We are sorry that we have failed you, but we cannot find your Daughter."

Demeter did not answer the Elder. She continued walking up and down the River bank. She did not eat, She did not drink, She did not sleep. She wandered about so long without rest that She was unrecognizable. Sometimes a hunter or gatherer would mistake her for Sasquatch and run hollering from the woods.

The flowers in the fields began to wither and die. The grass turned golden; when the wind moved through it, it made the sound rattlers make to warn you away. Streams and creeks dried up.

Coyote began to worry about the state of the world—especially about her empty belly—so she sought out Demeter. She found her sitting beside the Great Falls, Celilo, watching the huge red salmon leap into the air as they tried to swim up the falls.

"The salmon are returning," Coyote said.

Demeter said nothing. A chickadee flew onto her matted hair and began picking insects out of it.

Coyote raised an eyebrow. "That's quite a fashion statement," Coyote said. "Soon everyone will have that hair style. And those clothes. Beautiful."

Demeter slowly turned her head and looked at Coyote.

"Really. Could you show me how to do it?" Coyote asked.

Demeter stared at her.

"I've never had much sense when it comes to how I dress," Coyote said. "You know me, I'm too busy looking for something to eat to pay attention to what I look like. At the last gathering, Crow had to point out I had maggots in my teeth. Who knew? Carrion. Gets you every time."

Coyote detected a slight glimmer in Demeter's eyes. Was that recognition? A shiver of a smile?

"So you know what I did to distract them from the maggots in my teeth?" Coyote stood. "While I was picking my teeth with one hand, I did this with the other." She quickly lifted her skirt, revealing her naked vulva to Demeter.

Demeter could not help it. She began to laugh. And laugh.

Coyote dropped her skirt.

Demeter's belly laugh rocked the Great Falls. The fishers on the platforms stopped to look at her.

"My private parts are not *that* funny," Coyote said. "Although Crow and the others laughed themselves silly, too, come to think of it, when I showed them." Coyote lifted her skirt and looked down at her nakedness.

Demeter roared again.

Coyote smoothed down her skirt. "They are no funnier than anyone else's."

Demeter began picking the sticks out of her hair.

"Have you considered that maybe your Daughter is on her way home now?" Coyote asked.

"What do you mean?"

"She could be returning with the rest of the salmon," Coyote said.

"But once someone has been to the Salmon People, they never return."

"That is not always true," Coyote said.

Demeter stared at her. "Tell me what you've heard."

"Only that some can return to this world," she said. "Some are rescued. You are very powerful. I imagine you could find your Daughter and bring her back."

"But I don't know where or how."

Coyote nodded. "This I heard in a dream: To find your Daughter you must follow the ways of Snake, Cougar, and Bear. They will help you find the way. Once there, you must be prepared to offer the Salmon People something in exchange for your Daughter's release."

"I will do as you say," Demeter said. "Thank you, Coyote."

"You are welcome," Coyote said. She got up to leave. "And let's keep this little…joke…to ourselves, thank you very much."

Demeter nodded.

Coyote left.

"Snake," Demeter called out. "I am in need of your assistance."

Before the milk spilled across the night sky again, Snake appeared.

"What may I do for you?"

"Coyote says you can help me find my way to the Salmon People."

"Ah, that is a treacherous journey," Snake said. "Even for one like yourself. But I will show you."

Snake began dancing, slithering on the the ground, making shapes in the dirt. When She was finished, Demeter looked at the tracings in the Earth left by Snake's body and recognized them. They were the same curves as those made by Falling Creek.

"Thank you, Snake," Demeter said. "I am indebted to you."

Demeter walked and walked until She reached Falling Creek. She stood at its edge watching the stars on its skin until the sun came up. Then She followed the creek, only this time She traveled up, north, curving and winding through the fields and woods. After a time, her way was blocked by a sheer wall of stone. She tried going around it, but She kept losing her way. She knew She needed to stay near the river. Finally She sat down by the water and said, "Cougar, I am in need of your assistance."

Before the spine of the Universe held up the stars, Cougar padded into camp silently.

"How may I assist you?"

"I am going to the Salmon People to find my daughter, but my way is blocked," Demeter said. "Can you help me?"

Cougar looked across the river. Demeter followed his gaze. She could see a path going up the side of the waterfall. She had been so exhausted She had not even considered wading to the other side of the stream.

"Mother," Cougar said. "You are weary. Ride on my back. I will carry you across and up the waterfall."

Demeter accepted Cougar's kind offer. She clung to his back as he splashed through the water, then up the cliffs, past the waterfall, until the river was once again on relatively flat ground. Demeter got off the mountain lion.

"Thank you, Cougar," She said. "I am indebted to you."

Cougar walked back into the forest.

Demeter walked and walked. She was so exhausted that her rage dropped away, She was so exhausted all her grief softened, She was so exhausted She knew only that She was a woman on a mission.

After a time it felt like the river went on forever, and She could not go on another moment. Finally She sat by the river's edge and said, "Bear, I am in need of your assistance."

Before the stolen cornmeal dropped from the dog's mouth to become milky stars, Bear came crashing into Demeter's camp.

"How may I assist you?" Bear asked.

"I am searching for my Daughter where the Salmon People live," Demeter said. "But I have been traveling for a very long time and am getting nowhere. Can you help?"

Bear sat next to Demeter. "Yes," Bear said. "First, you must eat, you must drink, and you must sleep."

"I have no time for such things," Demeter said.

"You have time for all of that and more," Bear said.

Demeter did not have the strength to argue. She ate the food and drink Bear proffered. Then She lay her head in Bear's lap, and She fell to sleep. When She awakened, She ate the food and drink Bear proffered. Then She lay her head in Bear's lap and fell to sleep. They repeated this cycle again and again, until Demeter felt strength return to her body.

"Coyote told you you could rescue your Daughter," Bear said. "But she neglected to tell you that if you go to the Land of the Salmon People, even as powerful as you are, if you have not protected yourself ahead of time, you will not be able to leave either."

"I should have thought of that," Demeter said. "How should I protect myself?"

Bear held out a basket to Demeter. "Eat these."

Demeter reached her hand into the basket and came out with a handful of huckleberries. She laughed. "These simple precious berries?"

"They will protect you," Bear said, "and help you dream. You will need to dream the rest of the way to the Land of the Salmon People. Now sleep, my Mother."

Demeter closed her eyes and fell to sleep. She dreamed…

Meanwhile, Her Daughter had slipped and fallen into the water. She thought she would certainly drown, but the salmon and the river—which is life, after all—were fond of the girl. They had watched her grow from an infant to a girl to a teenager. She had run along the banks of the river, she had sung to the fish. So they could not let her drown. Instead, she became part of them.

She swam out into the Ocean with the rest of the salmon. She liked the Ocean very much. She would have stayed for a very long time except she kept hearing her Mother calling for her. So she returned to the Nch'I-Wana with the spawning salmon, and went up the river until she smelled the creek she had first fallen into and knew she was nearly home. She swam and swam, going with the flow of the other salmon, leaping when they leapt, resting when they rested, unable to get out of the water on her own until they all stepped out of the water together and into the arms of the elders of the Salmon People.

"We have a new daughter," the Salmon Elder said as she held out her hands to Her Daughter. "Welcome."

Her Daughter did not know what to say. She looked down and saw that her golden dress was now a beautiful crimson color.

"I would like to return to my Mother," Her Daughter said.

"We are sorry," the Salmon Elder said, "but that is not possible. So many people have forgotten our ways that we are losing more and more of the Salmon People. We need you here."

"But I don't belong," Her Daughter said.

"You do now," they told her.

For a long time, Her Daughter would not eat, drink, or sleep. This distressed the Salmon People greatly. But they could not let her go. Two of the men began vying for her attention. They wrestled and fought with one another until Her Daughter said, "I cannot abide war. If you have no better skills or imagination than to wage war against one another, I have no interest in either of you."

Her Daughter sat by the edge of the river most days and watched for her Mother. Other girls in the tribe came and sat with her. After a while, they became friends with Her Daughter and began showing her the ways of the Salmon People. One young man sat with her, too, and pointed out stars to her. At the Fire Dances, Her Daughter excelled, showing off her ability to control the fire sticks as she danced. She called herself Persephone now. Soon she no longer had much time to sit by the water and pine for her Mother. She became an expert basket-weaver, bread-maker, and storyteller. Still, she missed her Mother and wanted to see her again…

Demeter dreamed a map of the rest of the way to the Land of the Salmon People. It had been there all along: written in the shape of her body, in the breath in her lungs, in her love for Persephone. Rested and well-fed when She awakened to her empty camp, Demeter immediately set out. At mid-day, the threshold to the Land of the Salmon People appeared to Demeter. She ate a handful of huckleberries, then stepped over the threshold.

Immediately She saw Persephone preparing to sit down and feast. She gasped to see Her Daughter alive! Persephone had grown into a strong and beautiful young woman. Demeter shouted with joy. Her Daughter turned and saw her Mother. They ran into each other's arms. The Salmon People watched the two women embrace. After a few minutes, Demeter pulled away from Persephone but kept a hold of her hand.

"I have brought you huckleberries," Demeter said, holding out the basket to her daughter. Persephone took a handful of berries and put them in her mouth.

"And I have baked you bread," Persephone said, holding out to her mother the braided bread she had brought over to the feast. Demeter gratefully ate a piece of the bread her daughter had made.

"I thank you for taking care of Persephone," Demeter said to the Salmon People. "She left me a girl, and now she is a grown woman. Now I am taking her home."

Persephone's young man stepped forward. "Do you wish to return to your former home?"

Persephone looked into her Mother's face, then back at the Salmon People. "I am at home in both worlds," she said. "It is a difficult choice."

Demeter could not bear the thought of never seeing Her Daughter again.

"If you will let her leave with me," Demeter said, "I promise we will teach your ways to the world. To keep the waters pristine, the air clear, the rivers unblocked. We will teach the people to respect you, to sing to you, to celebrate you again in all ways."

"It is Persephone's decision," one Elder said.

"I will go with my mother part of the year and return here for part of each year," Persephone said, "to learn more of the ways of the Salmon People."

The Elders nodded. "This bargain we accept. Let us feast to commemorate this day!"

Demeter and Persephone feasted, danced, and sang with the Salmon People for many days. Then they prepared to leave the Land of the Salmon People.

The Salmon People embraced Persephone and Demeter and said their farewells. Then Demeter and Persephone stepped over the threshold and found themselves standing by Falling Creek in the exact spot where Her Daughter had fallen. Crow called to them from above.

"It is good to see Mother and Daughter reunited," Crow said.

"It is good to see you again, too, Crone Mother," Persephone said.

Demeter and Persephone splashed in the creek together, then ran up the hill and across the fields, hand in hand, wildflowers springing up from their footsteps.

Mystai Tasks

How do you feel about this myth? When reading it now, do you relate more to Demeter or Persephone, or one of the other beings in the story? If you've done the mysteries before, are your feelings different this year? For instance, some years I feel myself drawn to Demeter; other years, I feel like Baubo or Coyote. Have you taken your own trip to the Underworld? Did you receive any gifts from this journey? Write about your own pilgrimage and explore those gifts.

Record dreams here.

A Little Herstory, or How to Become Mythwise

I who am the beauty of the green earth and the white moon among the stars and the mysteries of the water, I call upon your soul to arise and come unto me. For I am the soul of nature that gives life to the universe.
—Doreen Valiente, adapted by Starhawk

Our ancestors understood the power of story. Scholars tell us myths were created by people to explain the unexplainable Natural forces they encountered every day. I think they understood Nature a great deal more than we do. Story was about honoring, celebrating, documenting and often personifying those Natural processes. A good storyteller knew (and knows) places talk to her. The land tells its story through a storyteller. Stories do not imbue a place with meaning; place imbues the story with meaning. Stories were articulations of the land, of Nature. Humans were an active *bodily* part of Nature. As people told these stories over and over, the tales began to resonate more deeply; the magic and meaning of countless tellings during ceremony or around campfires clung to every word and intonation.

Stories have power.

The conquering hordes knew this. Whenever one group of people took over another group of people, they most often incorporated the local god/desses into their own schema of the world. When the patriarchal conquerors who worshipped the desert gods rode into town, they, too, incorporated the local god/desses into their pantheons. But first they tweaked the stories. Especially the goddess stories. Powerful women from an egalitarian peaceful society were not acceptable in a male-dominated warrior society. The goddesses had to be demoralized and stripped of their power while their myths were ostensibly retained. The Goddess was broken into pieces, raped, humiliated, and denigrated. For instance, Hera was mother to all, *the* Great Goddess to many, especially protective of women's sexuality. Once the Greeks got hold of her, she became Zeus's jealous shrewish wife.

Then there's Athena. According to Patricia Monaghan, her name was "so ancient that it has never been translated."[16] Most likely Minoan, she may have been a household goddess, guardian of the home and all who dwelled within. Once she made that trip to Greece, she was suddenly a warrior goddess who popped out of her "daddy's" head one day. That little twist on the myth erases any connection she may have had with the Goddess religion, doesn't it? She's not even *born* from a female!

Medusa became an ugly horrible creature who could kill with a glance. Originally she was the "serpent-goddess of the Libyan Amazons, representing 'female wisdom.'"[17] While Athena was depicted as Medusa's enemy in the Greek tales, Medusa and Athena may actually have been different aspects of the same goddess.

The goddess Demeter and Her Mysteries most likely originated in Crete rather than the patriarchal Greece. Greek poet Hesiod (c. 750 B.C.E.) and Greek historian Diodorus (c. 50 B.C.E.) linked her with Crete,[18] while Greek historian Herodotus (c. 485 B. C.E.-425 B.C.E.) claimed Demeter and her rituals came from Egypt via Crete, "where Demeter was the daughter of the Minoan goddess Rhea."[19] She "traveled" from a peaceful, goddess-worshipping, Nature-loving society into a patriarchal intellectual warrior society. What a trip!

Demeter was "once the Mother of the Great Triangle of Life, the Mystery of the Universe, complete in all Her parts: Creator, Preserver, Destroyer."[20] As with most of the goddesses from other cultures that were incorporated into the Greek pantheon, Demeter was split into various other goddesses which contained aspects of her original powerful self. She became Persephone the maiden, Demeter the mother, and Hecate the crone. Or Persephone and Hecate became aspects of the Dark Goddess while Demeter became "only" the mother.

In early societies when the cycles of Nature were revered and often personified as the Goddess, the cycles of life were better understood. The Dark Goddess—the aspect of the Great Goddess that ruled over death, transformation, menstruation, rebirth—was worshipped. Power and healing were available to those who understood that darkness held the potential for renewal.

Whether you view the story of Demeter and Persephone as primarily an agricultural myth, a blood mystery, or a story about the cycles of our lives, at its center Demeter and Persephone take deep, dark, and unexpected journeys which bring them grief, transformation, and a new *sense* of their lives. Mara

Lynn Keller believes "one of the central precepts of the ancient Mysteries was 'know thyself.'"[21]

It is still essential to "know thyself" and understand the stories we tell and the stories we hear. The conquerors of the early matrifocal cultures knew enough to rewrite, reshape, and distort the "herstory" of the goddesses. What we believe is true shapes our world in many ways. If we as a people believe Nature is inanimate, for instance, existing only for our exploitation, then we as a people will exploit and destroy Nature. The patriarchal conquerors originally came from the desert believing in a punishing sky god. As their influence has spread across the globe, so has the desert: Global warming is turning our planet into a desert.

So let's change the story.

Mystai Tasks

Draw the the mother of life, the Mystery of the Universe, complete in all Her parts: Creatrix, Preserver, Destroyer. (Blank pages are at the end of the chapter.) Write about your experiences today or about your feelings regarding the Great Mother.

Record dreams here.

What Happened in Eleusis?

Demeter bestowed on us two gifts, the greatest gifts of all:
first the fruits of the earth...and second, the mysteries.
—Isocrates (4th c. B.C.E.)

Demeter was the goddess of the upperworld, the Earth. After Persephone's journey to the Underworld, Persephone became goddess—or Queen—of the Underworld. Earth/Moon, Light/Dark, outer/inner, mother/daughter, seed/fruit, summer/winter are recognized and honored in this myth. Autumnal Equinox, when these Mysteries took place, is the moment when light and dark are balanced, just before the scales (of Libra) are tipped toward darkness again (only to be tipped back toward the light after Spring Equinox).

Although we don't know the "mystery" of the Eleusinian Mysteries, we do have a fair idea of what happened during much of the nine-day celebration, "culled from veiled contemporary accounts, obscure literary references, the satire of playwrights and the prejudiced accounts of early Christian writers seeking to justify suppression of the mysteries."[22]

The celebration may (or may not) have started on September 14, nine days from Autumnal Equinox. Accounts vary on what happened during those days, and I will discuss them in greater length in subsequent chapters. For our purposes here, these were the basics:

On the first day, September 14, the priestesses of Demeter (called Melissae) walk the fourteen miles from Athens to Eleusis. It is most likely a beautiful day, the sky a pale pale blue, the ground coriander-colored; a light breeze carries the scent of olive trees up the road that curved snakelike through the countryside. The priestesses carry the *hiera*—sacred objects of the Goddess—in beautiful wide baskets on their heads. The Melissae can feel the excitement all around them, vibrating up from the ground and through the soles of their feet. *It is time for the Mysteries.*

On the second day, the Mystai—the initiates who participated in the Lesser Mysteries earlier in the year—stand apart from the crowd while an official reads aloud the requirements for attendance at the celebration. All slaves, women, children, men are welcome, as long as they have not killed anyone.

On the third day, a herald calls out, "To the sea, initiates, to the sea!" The Mystai hurry to the Aegean. They take off their clothes, step into the cool pure water, and bathe themselves as they pray. When they come out of the water, they put on new clothes.

The Mystai spend the fourth day in prayer. They make bloodless sacrifices and promises for their new lives. During the following day, latecomers are allowed to join the Mysteries; the healer Asclepius is honored.

On the sixth day, September 19, the Mystai begin their journey down the Sacred Road to Eleusis. On the way, community members line the streets and walk along with the initiates, ridiculing them and revealing their secrets. Someone dressed as Baubo lifts her skirt and exposes herself to the Mystai.

The Mystai rest and prepare for the Mysteries on the seventh day. The Mysteries begin that night in the Telesterion, Demeter's temple, and continue on the eighth night.

On the ninth day the community and the Mystai—now no longer initiates—honor the dead and make offerings to the goddesses. Although the nine-day celebration is over for this year, the Mysteries continue all through the seasons in the Natural world and in the bodies of those who experienced them.

Those who had been initiated in the Mysteries and spoke about their experiences said they felt transformed and peaceful; it was a joyful, healing, and profound event in their lives.

How do we make these Mysteries relevant and part of our own lives today?

Follow the story.

Mystai Tasks

Express the mystery in some way here. Draw it, collage it, write about it. Sing it. (Blank pages are at the end of the chapter.)

How do the natural cycles reflect the story of Demeter and Persephone in your part of the world? i.e. when are flowers blooming? When are fruits ripe? When are plants dying or going dormant? Be specific and detailed until you understand the cycles of the story and how they relate to the cycles of Nature.

Record dreams here.

How Should You Prepare?

Begin with the stirring,
begin with the stirring
in your own dark center,
begin...
—Gwendolyn Endicott

The journey of a thousand miles begins with one step.
—Lao Tzu (570-490 B.C.E.)

As a participant in The Salmon Mysteries, you have a responsibility to take care of yourself—particularly during the nine days. Try to eat healthy, sleep well, and avoid intoxicants or mood-altering substances. (Generally speaking, most people today don't understand the sacred use of intoxicants and instead become addicted to them.)

Spend at least five minutes a day in silent meditation. If you can manage it, spend fifteen minutes a day. Put your box of *hiera* in front of you as you meditate. (More on this later.) Over time, the *hiera* become a mnemonic for your Mystery experiences. If you have trouble staying still and taking time for yourself, chant as you meditate: OM AH HUM, or OM TARA TUTARE TURE SOHA. Or whatever mantra you prefer. This will help you remain grounded and present.

If you're celebrating the Mysteries with a group, prepare together and talk about what your goals are for the celebration or what you hope to accomplish. Don't intellectualize it too much. You want to be open to the mystery of it all.

If shamanic journeying is a part of what you do, journey with your Helping Spirits to ancient Eleusis or to the Goddess Demeter. Ask if you should be on the lookout for certain signs or gifts during the coming days. Find out if a particular power animal or Helping Spirit will be your guide during this time.

If you get a chance, do a walking meditation every day. Walk and chant to yourself as you keep your mind relatively empty. Do this for approximately fifteen minutes a day if possible.

Most of us are overstimulated, so keep the television off as much as possible during these nine days. Avoid advertisements. Try to drive less. Use your computer less. Overall, be quiet, still, and contemplative. Create an altar or sacred space just for the Mysteries.

Record your experiences each day. Again, write them, draw them, make clay shapes or collages out of them.

Doing is less important than experiencing the process. This is all about *being*.

Before the Mysteries begin, find images for a collage. If you plan on doing more than one collage over the nine days, get lots of images! If not, find images for a collage on the Day of Mystery. Rip out pictures from magazines you like, or bring along entire magazines. Old greeting cards work well, too. Also get poster board. If you're doing several collages over the week, you might want several smaller pieces of poster board.

Mostly, try to stay present, in your body, experiencing all that is going on in and around you. Don't try to control or anticipate the Mysteries and your experience of them. If you come to the Mysteries believing you must feel a certain way or experience a certain thing, you will be disappointed. Try to go with the flow. Begin with a beginner's mind and stay a beginner throughout the nine days.

Mystai Tasks

Do a collage representing your preparation here or on a separate sheet. Do a meditation in preparation for the Mysteries and then color or draw your experience. (Blank pages are at the end of the chapter.)

Read Day Eight and Day of Mystery (pages 105-116, excluding the Mystai Tasks). Make a list of anything you need to get ahead of time for the Night of the Mysteries and for the Feast. Remember the food should have meaning, either culturally, geographically, or metaphorically. Plan your menu here. Take notes about what you want.

Record dreams here.

Day One: Day of Commitment

Let no part of me
ever be separate again
Let no part of you
be unknown to me
Earth of my body
Body of the Earth
—Karen Zeiders

Eleusinian Mysteries

For our purposes, the Eleusinian Mysteries will begin September 14th. According to most historians, this was the day that Demeter's priestesses gathered together her sacred objects—the *hiera*. They put them in baskets and carried them to Eleusis. What was in the baskets? Z. Budapest says the items were "a comb, a symbol of Aphrodite, a mirror, a snake figure or live snake (for rebirth), wheat, and barley."[23]

Scholars have suggested that the contents of the basket were "a replica of the womb, or a phallus, or a snake, or cakes in the shape of genital organs."[24] Demetra George writes that some scholars believed the objects were "various sorts of cakes, a serpent, pomegranates, leaves and stalks, poppies, and a model of a woman's genitals."[25]

Whatever was in the beautifully-made baskets, the priestesses of Demeter carried them as they walked the flower-strewn Sacred Road to Eleusis.

The Salmon Mysteries

This part of the myth occurred before my reimagining of the story begins. I don't explain how Demeter and Persephone must have prepared for their journey which began in spring. What do you think? How does a goddess prepare for creation?

Mystai Tasks

As you prepare to begin the Mysteries on September 14 (or whatever date you chose), imagine yourself as a Mystes and Melissa, Persephone and Demeter. What would you take on a transformative journey to the Underworld? As Demeter, you know what would help your daughter; as Persephone, you know what you need. Journey or meditate on this.

_____
_____
_____
_____
_____
_____
_____
_____
_____
_____
_____
_____

Find yourself a small basket with a lid, or a box with a lid. Don't feel like you need to buy anything. This isn't about consumption, this is about being in your present environment and letting your intuition guide you. Write about the process here and/or put a photograph of it here. Walk around your home (inside or out) and ask the Natural forces to help you find items to guide you on your journey. What do you hear, what do you see? A bird's feather? A rock? A plastic toy bear? You don't need to fill the basket. You can choose one item, or something for each of the four directions (east, south, west, north) or the elements (air, fire, water, earth). What will help you remember you are on a sacred journey? What would you like to lay at the feet of the Goddess? Think of the Mysteries as you collect these items.

Write about your small basket or box. What did you pick to put in it? Why? When you are finished, put the items in your basket. Make up your own blessing and bless the objects (or use mine below). Sit quietly for a moment with the basket and the items you've chosen. For the rest of the nine days, try to keep the basket near you. Paste in a photo if you like or draw your basket.

Blessing the Sacred Objects:
Great Mother, Bless these objects large and small
As they help me answer the Call.
Guide me to the Sacred Way
As I begin on this blessed day.
With harm to none, may it be done!

How are you committed to this process? Why are you doing this?

_____

_____

_____

_____

_____

_____

_____

_____

_____

Also, do you have everything you need for the Feast or do you have plans to get the items?

_____

_____

_____

_____

_____

_____

_____

_____

_____

_____

_____

_____

Record dreams here.

Day Two: Day of Gathering

Now, while we are dancing
Come! Join us!
Sweet joy, revelry,
Bright light!
—Sappho, translated by Charoula

The Eleusinian Mysteries

On the second day the celebrations officially began with an announcement of the qualifications needed in order to join the Mysteries. All were welcomed, as long as they had never killed anyone (unless the killing had been expiated). The community and the Mystai gathered to hear the announcement.

The Salmon Mysteries

In our story, this is when Demeter and Persephone walk in the fields; Demeter creates while Persephone follows close at her heels. Companions run alongside them.

Mystai Tasks

You have now been officially invited to the Mysteries! What do you require of yourself in order to complete this journey? Think about what you want from yourself during this process; then write or draw how you feel.

If you can today, try to do something with your community. You don't need to arrange anything special—you've already got a bit to do in the next nine days. Harvest festivals abound at this time of year. Attend one of them. Watch how people celebrate. How does it feel to be with these people as they celebrate? Do you feel part of it or apart from it? Imagine your entire community is gathered together to begin a journey to the Goddess. How would that celebration be different?

Record dreams here.

Day Three: Day of Purification

Deep inside me at my core
is where my Mother lives.
—Cassia Berman

The Eleusinian Mysteries

The herald cried out, "Go to the sea, initiates." The Mystai gathered at the shore of the Aegean Sea, dropped all that they carried with them on the beach, took off their clothes, and performed purification rituals while dousing themselves with sea water. When they were finished, they stepped into the new clothes they had brought with them.

The Salmon Mysteries

In our story, Persephone runs down to the creek. She loses her balance and falls into the water. She has always wanted to see the world of the salmon, and now she is swimming in it. This is when she could drown and die. Those beginning moments when we first begin the descent are always the most perilous, when we could lose our bodies or minds. But the transmutation has begun. What could kill her—the water—now becomes her guardian. She is transformed by the water and becomes one of the Salmon People.

Persephone's descent into the Underworld, which in our story is the water and the Land of the Salmon, represents many things. Demeter as the grain goddess is the seed and Persephone is the fruit. They are the same, only at different stages in the process. Persephone's descent can also be interpreted as a metaphor for menarche and the awakening of Persephone's sexuality. In the classical Greek version, Persephone's introduction to her own sexuality comes through rape.

I thought a long time about whether I should include the abduction and rape in The Salmon Mysteries. This part of the story has always troubled me, yet in real life, Greek women were dealing with an oppressive patriarchal society where they were seen as little more than property. Rape and oppression were a part of their existence. Through the Demeter and Persephone story, women would be able to ritually live through the horrible events of their lives and come out on the other side transformed and powerful. The classical version of the Demeter and Persephone myth delineates the horror of the patriarchy and how to survive it. We still live in an oppressive state where Nature and women are raped and defiled daily. Don't we need a story that demonstrates we can live through it?

I kept coming back to the idea that we become, as a society, the stories we tell. I want stories where the kidnapper and rapist does *not* get the girl, so to speak. I agree with Mara Lynn Keller who writes that "the Mysteries of Demeter and Persephone embodied the values of the relatively peaceful farming and trading mother-clan societies of the Goddess-preeminent Neolithic, before the sacrifice of sons in war became common practice as patriarchal warrior clans forced their way to power."[26]

As a child, I learned a history which took for granted that people had always waged war and murdered one another. As an adult when I first studied the scientific, archaeological, and mythological evidence that some of our ancestors may have lived in peaceful egalitarian matrifocal communities for thousands of year before the warrior culture took over, I was stunned and ecstatic. This was a story I needed! I could envision this other culture. It was something to strive for in the future. When I read the classical Demeter and Persephone story, I felt defined by oppression.

So I left out the rape and abduction in The Salmon Mysteries. Persephone's descent, her transformation, occurs when she falls into the water. This fall can symbolize the plunge a person needs to make into her own emotional identity so that she can truly know herself. She travels to the ocean of her being. If she lets herself *feel*, she will become herself once again, changed by the experience but still herself.

Meanwhile, Demeter looks frantically for her daughter. She asks Crow to help her. In the classical Demeter and Persephone myth, Hecate helps reunite mother and daughter. Hecate has a complex herstory, to say the least. Some scholars say she was originally Egyptian, others say Thracian. She was worshipped as the goddess of midwives, crossroads, the moon, and the Underworld. She was the Crone goddess. Her worshipers left food offerings at the trivia—the crossroads. Because she is a goddess of the Underworld, she is often associated with Halloween. When I picture her, I envision the stereotypical version of the witch: dressed all in black with a tall pointed hat.

Like Hecate, the crow has a complex mythic lineage. Because crow is a carrion-eater, she is associated with the Underworld. In North American mythology, Crow is sometimes creator/creatrix, sometimes trickster—or both. He brings light to humans; she makes order in the universe. (I am not distinguishing between crow and raven here.) Crows sat at the omphalos at Delphi[27] and helped to carry prophetic messages of the Pythia.

Crow is a perfect companion for Hecate. In our story, she *is* Hecate. As the goddess of midwives and protector of women, Hecate guides women and gives them perspective on their journeys. This is what she does in our story, even though she does not tell Demeter where she can find Persephone.

Even though we encounter Crow only twice in The Salmon Mysteries, she is a guardian for Demeter and Persephone, safe-guarding both women as they each come to their own crossroads.

All of us find ourselves at a crossroads or on a descent into the Underworld at one time or another because of financial difficulties, illness, a death or deep loss. Crow/Hecate knows these roads, is familiar with this territory, and can help us get some perspective and direction.

Demeter collapses into despair when she and Crow cannot find Persephone. She asks "Why me," a familiar cry to those of us who have been ill, lost a loved one, been homeless, penniless. No one answers Demeter because there is no answer to this question. Some manner of suffering happens to all of us, often for no apparent reason.

Mystai Tasks

On this third day of the Mysteries, go down to a nearby stream, river, pool, ocean. Take with you a set of clothes you have chosen that represents a "new beginning" for you. You may choose all white, which many scholars believe the Mystai wore, or something gold (or yellow) like Persephone's dress before she fell into the water; you can add a red scarf to it later after the Day of Mystery to represent

Persephone's (and your own) transformation. Maybe you want something purple or bright green. It doesn't have to be store-bought new or even new to you, just pick something which gives you a little hiccup of excitement at the thought of wearing it. Make sure it's comfortable and something you can wear performing a number of tasks. I would suggest having an accessory which you can put on and take off easily. You won't wear the entire outfit during the nine days, but you might want to wear part of it—such as a scarf.

When you go to the river take a container of water and a towel. Most streams, rivers, pools, and oceans are not clean enough for you to actually bathe in. If you know a body of water is safe, go for it! Otherwise, stand at the edge of the water. Wash your hands and face in the water you brought as you recite the purification chant (from one you've made up or use mine below). Pour any leftover water into the river. Then dry yourself. If you're someplace private, take off your "old" clothes and put on your "new." (If you aren't any place private, wear the new clothes to your water spot.) As you dress in your new clothes, remember this change of clothes represents your change—your willingness to "know thyself."

Purification Rite:

Demeter and Persephone,
With this sacred water
Purify and heal me.
I am Mother, I am Daughter,
Lover of all I see:
Sky, mountain, river, and field
Mother/Daughter, blessed me!
Give me power I can wield.
Purify and heal me, blessed be!

Our ancestors viewed shorelines as sacred thresholds, places that were betwixt and between. Water is the elixir of life, sacred and precious. You are not purifying yourself because your body is dirty. The purification rites are part of the process of altering your consciousness, of altering your being. Recognize with these purification rites that you are a precious being, you are a beginner, and you are ready to change to become your true self. You want to be full of your self!

Also, say a prayer to Crow/Hecate. Ask her to guide you as you travel down the sometimes treacherous road of your life.

How was your Day of Purification? Journal about it here. Draw any part of it on the blank pages at the end of the chapter.

Record dreams here.

Day Four: Day of Coyote

Laugh deep in the body,
laugh down to your soul.
She considers it an invocation,
swoops in the open window,
lets you near Her.
—Judith Sornberger

The Eleusinian Mysteries

The community participants and Mystai spent the fourth day in prayer, reciting special prayers for women and children. They made further sacrifices to the Goddess. Originally these sacrifices were bloodless. Some scholars believe the use of pigs as sacrifices was added to the Mysteries later and was not originally a part of them. Demeter was the "goddess of the plants that feed us. Because of her connection with growth, Demeter was always worshiped in fireless sacrifices, demanding all offerings in their natural state."[28]

The Salmon Mysteries

In our story, Demeter wanders the countryside grieving over the loss of her daughter. She doesn't eat, drink, bathe, or sleep. She is sometimes mistaken for Sasquatch.

Sasquatch, or Bigfoot, is an important character in the Pacific Northwest. Europeans encountered the big hairy being when they first moved out here, but Native Americans already had a history with Sasquatch, who was called by many different names, including Bukwus, the Wild Man, and Dzonoqua, the Wild Woman. Some called them Seeahtlks, great hunters who had a "vulgar sense of humor."[29]

Some other names of Bigfoot-like beings include "Wampus, a legendary monster of the forest in the Oregon Cascades; Xi'lgo and Yi'dyi'tay, the Tillamook Wild Woman and Wild Man, At'at'ahila among the Chinookans; Qah-lin-me, devourer of Yakamas; and Omah, of the Yurok to the south."[30] Today many coastal and forest Native Americans believe in Bigfoot just as they would any of the animals we look up in field guides. Their encounters with Sasquatch often put them in danger, yet the experiences were frequently shamanic in nature, leaving the "experiencer" with powers s/he hadn't had before.[31] It was not an encounter many sought since a sighting of Sasquatch often preceded danger or was a message from the spirits suggesting something was off-kilter: life out of balance.

Native Americans are not alone in their belief in Bigfoot. In the county where I live, the county commissioners passed an ordinance in 1969 protecting Bigfoot. It became illegal to shoot or harm Bigfoot in any way. It is legal to shoot just about anything where I live, so this law is rather astonishing. Bigfoot hunters descended upon this county after several area sightings in the sixties, determined to be the one to bag Sasquatch. (Some believers said the only way to prove Bigfoot was real was to kill one.) The county commissioners were probably afraid someone would mistake a Bigfoot hunter for a Bigfoot, so they enacted the protective ordinance.

To many worshipers, Demeter was a grain goddess. It was she who brought agriculture (and therefore settled culture) to the people. Yet in her grief, she comes to be mistaken for Sasquatch—for a Wild Woman. Her grief pushes her into a descent to her Wild Woman nature. Is this a true natural Wild Woman or someone who has been pushed beyond her limits? Seeing Demeter in such a state surely meant life was out of balance. The grass withers and browns. The flowers die. Demeter is not tending to her Earth. She ends up sitting by the River where the fish are returning to spawn. Despite her grief, despite her apparent disregard for creating, life continues *in* the Big River—at least for now.

This is when Demeter encounters Coyote. In the classical version, Demeter wanders into Eleusis, disguised, and takes a job as a nursemaid to a queen's son. Baubo (whose name means belly) tries to console the grieving mother, but Demeter ignores her. Then Baubo does the unexpected: She raises her skirts and exposes her vulva. Demeter smiles, and then she starts to laugh until her belly shakes. Soon after, she is reunited with her daughter. The laughter melted away her depression and helped facilitate her healing.

Clarissa Pinkola Estés has her own version of the encounter between Demeter and Baubo:

> And as she [Demeter] leaned her aching body against the cool stone of the well, along came a woman, or rather a sort of woman. And this woman danced up to Demeter wiggling her hips in a way suggesting sexual intercourse, and shaking her breasts in her little dance. And when Demeter saw her, she could not help but smile just a little.
>
> The dancing female was very magical indeed, for she had no head whatsoever, and her nipples were her eyes and her vulva was her mouth. It was through this lovely mouth that she began to regale Demeter with some nice juicy jokes. Demeter began to smile, and then chuckled, and then gave a full belly laugh.[32]

Baubo's significance in the Demeter and Persephone myth indicates she was probably once a powerful goddess in her own right, stripped of her status by patriarchal storytellers. She represented women's bawdy, uncontrollable humor and sexuality. Pretty scary stuff for the patriarchy. Yet she couldn't be completely denigrated because her power lay in her biology: a belly laugh is healing. Being in our bodies and dancing, laughing, and shaking our "private parts" is awe-inspiring, grounding, and sensual.

Demeter had essentially left her body (her body being the Earth), and her laughter brought her straight back into her being. Baubo helped her do that. In our story, Coyote is Baubo's counterpart.

Coyote, like Crow, is another ineffable character in the North American landscape. Coyote stories are as ubiquitous as stars in the Milky Way (and Coyote supposedly created the Milky Way when he opened the lid to a pot and the stars escaped). Coyote is creatrix and trickster, responsible for great tribulations and ceaseless wonders. In other words, Coyote can be blamed or celebrated for just about anything, and in the West, she often is. Missing a cat? Must be a coyote. A sheep. Get the shotgun and kill that ki-yote. In some Northwest Indian legends, Coyote put the salmon in the Nch'I-Wana and showed the

Indians how to fish. (Coyote may have had ulterior motives; everyone knows Coyote is always hungry.)

In our story Coyote sits by Demeter and tries to coax her out of her grief. When she lifts her skirts, Demeter laughs. Coyote sees Demeter is coming back into her body. At that point—once Demeter is embodied again—Coyote shares a dream she had, imparting shamanic information to Demeter by telling her who will be her guides on her quest to find her daughter.

Mystai Tasks

On this day, you should take time out to pray. You don't have to pray to a deity, certainly, especially if you don't believe in one! I think of prayer as a song I sing to myself and the Universe. I chant (pray) as a way to center myself, to ground myself in the here and now. This is another way of deepening as you follow the path of the Mysteries.

Think of something you can sacrifice to this process. To sacrifice means to make sacred. Is there a habit you can "make sacred" by letting it go, giving it up? Your body is your temple, goddess, divinity, world: Are you harming yourself in some way? Can you let it go today? Release it, give it up.

_____

_____

_____

_____

Changing is difficult for us. We grow accustomed to our ruts, no matter how deep and harmful they are. We want to be habitual. We like cycles. But change is possible. See if you can exchange a harmful cycle or habit for a healing cycle.

_____

_____

_____

_____

The Trickster, either as Coyote or the bawdy Baubo, is often a character in our own real life stories, whether we like it or not. The way of the Trickster is rarely comfortable. Coyote teaches us that life isn't a puzzle we can solve. It isn't something we can control. Go with the flow, Coyote tells us, and laugh even as you're falling.

Coyote teaches us about surviving. More than that, Coyote thrives, even in trying times. This trickster survivor is certainly not appreciated by our culture. During some years our government kills 100,000 coyotes, mostly with M-44s put in meat. When the coyote bites into the meat, the M-44s explode in her face. Hunters (and other people) regularly kill an additional 300,000 coyotes each year. Despite this yearly slaughter, coyotes thrive—or maybe because of it. Scientists have discovered that when the coyote population is stressed (for instance when lots of coyotes are killed in a territory) the females have *more* pups. A pair normally has two to three pups a year, but during those killing times, they breed more and have seven to ten pups.

Coyote teaches us that we can survive the worst of times until the best of times roll around again.

Write about your process today. Or draw it. Do both, especially if one or the other makes you uncomfortable. (Blank pages at the end of the chapter.)

Record dreams here.

Day Five: Day of Snake

Movement is my medicine. Rhythm is our universal mother tongue.
It's the language of the soul.
—Gabrielle Roth

The mystery is always of a body
The mystery is always of a body of a woman
...The mystery of the mystery is being woman
...the mystery is always of the body in the body of a woman.
—Hélène Cixous

The Eleusinian Mysteries

On this day, a procession was held to honor Asclepius, the divine physician. (Apparently he showed up at the Mysteries late, but they let him in anyway. So this day was set aside to allow latecomers to join.) Those who were in need of healing may have incubated dreams at nearby temples, then shared what they learned with the community on this day. Asclepius is symbolized by a rod with twin snakes twined around it, "borrowed" from his predecessor the goddess Hygeia. (I'm sure you've seen this symbol in your physician's office or on a prescription pad.) "Central to his cult was the use of dream incubation," Demetra George writes, "and he was honored as the god of 'Nootherapia' (mind healing) who purified and healed the entire being, both body and mind, using exclusively mental means and the spiritual power of the divine."[33]

The initiates did not join this procession and celebration. In seclusion they may have performed rituals related to Demeter's grief.

The Salmon Mysteries

In our story, Demeter calls for help from Snake. When Snake arrives, she first acknowledges that Demeter's task is great. Then Snake dances. This is how she accesses the information Demeter needs. She gets down and dirty, literally. When she is finished, a map remains in the dirt. Snake *embodied* the way. And the way is by the water. Demeter has to return to the place where it all started. To the Source.

Snakes have been linked with women and the Goddess throughout recorded time. Because the snake periodically sheds its skin, it was associated with the moon and its phases and a woman's menstrual cycle. Demeter "had a snake, called Kychrens, as her attendant at the temple of Eleusis."[34] In a cave in southern France, an ancient artist painted a giant snake with a woman's body; they've dated this artwork to somewhere within the years of 40,000-26,000 B.C.E. This is not the earliest or only example of a serpent goddess in human art. Archaeologist Marija Gimbutas and artist Buffie Johnson each documented ancient representations of the snake goddess in cultures all over the planet.

Vicki Noble writes:

> Everywhere in the ancient prepatriarchal world, the Great Snake represented the cosmic creative forces of the Divine Feminine. Australian Aborigines call her the Rainbow Serpent; Paleolithic cave dwellers made an image of her as a winged dragon...In India, Tantric worshipers honor the Goddess (and women as her earthly incarnation) through celebration of the kundalini energy, the female serpent power that moves spontaneously through the body when aroused by sexual or yogic practices.[35]

In Ohio, ancient Native Americans created a snake effigy on a cliff overlooking a creek. It is still there, over 1300 feet long and twenty feet wide, curving along the ground. I was lucky enough to visit it and was amazed at how indescribably beautiful it is—and mythic in a totally physical way. The snake is made from earth: The snake is Earth and the Earth is Snake.

In Crete, from where Demeter most likely hails, the Serpent Goddess is pre-eminent. You've probably seen a duplicate of one of the small statues found in Knossos. The goddess is bare-breasted, her arms outstretched with a writhing snake in each hand. Her waist is tiny with a kind of apron tied around it (indicative of her status as priestess); beneath the apron, a layered skirt falls. Her eyes are black and hypnotic, as if she is in a trance or attempting to get you to fall into one. The power of her gaze has not diminished in nearly 4,000 years.

Snake dances were performed by our ancestors and are still danced today. The Hopi ritually dance with rattlesnakes. It is no surprise that Demeter had a snake guarding her temple in Eleusis or that she calls upon a snake for help. Snake is the embodiment of the female shaman. She comes when she is called, and she dances the healing dance.

Because snakes were associated with women and the Goddess for tens of thousands of years, it should come as no surprise that the snake was then demonized by the patriarchy and in particular the Christian church. In fact, it is the Serpent in the Judeo-Christian mythos who causes the downfall of humankind. Eve desired Serpent knowledge—that deep, dark, bloody, intuitive, fiery female wisdom. In the patriarchy, the very existence of any wise women was denied and forbidden.

Today, many women fear snakes. Some cannot bear to even look at pictures of snakes. Is it because we fear our own power and the consequences of it? Snakes and women are forever linked in the Western mind with humankind's expulsion from Eden. With their bellies sliding seductively against the Earth, snakes remind us that the hidden knowledge the patriarchy tries to keep from us is still accessible through our bodies and our connection with the Earth.

Mystai Tasks

For you on this day, think about what needs healing in your life. Then dance it. Don't intellectualize it. Don't think about it any more. Don't write about it. Dance it. Through the dance, you will find the way to yourself and the profound hidden knowledge that lies within you. Everything you require is on this Earth. You are a part of this Earth; therefore everything you need is in your body. Shed what you don't need, just as the snake sheds her skin. Move out of the old, the destructive, the unnecessary. Dance into what you truly need and into who you truly are. If you can't dance with your legs, dance with your arms, your head.

Be in your body. Feel your body and the ground beneath your feet as you dance.

Dance outside if you can. Take a walk in the woods. Find your own path. Notice the plants, trees, birds. Not from a distance. *Be* with them. *Be* a part of the Natural world—because you *are* a part of it, no matter how disconnected you may feel. Dance with all that you see, hear, smell. The Wind will love it! The Earth will love it. Heal! Celebrate!

Try to incubate a healing dream tonight. "During transitional times," Vicki Noble writes, "…temples were built for initiates to 'incubate' healing dreams. Such temples were presided over by priestesses of the Goddess Hygeia or later the priests of healing gods, such as Asclepius."[36] In Greek mythology, Hygeia, the Goddess of Health, and Panacea, the Goddess of Cures, are Asclepius's daughters. Yet they were ancient goddesses, around long before Asclepius. Make your bedroom your healing temple. Add something to your altar in honor of Hygeia, Panacea, Asclepius—or any other healing entity to whom you turn during times of illness or stress. Put a pad of paper and pen within your reach near the bed. As you go to sleep, ask for a healing dream. When you awaken, write down whatever you've dreamed, whether you understand it or not. Don't try to analyze it; take it as a gift from the Divine and know that the healing has already begun.

Write about your experiences today.

Record dreams here.

Day Six: Procession Day

You cannot travel the path until you have become the path.
—Gautama Buddha (563-483 B.C.E.)

Glorious it is when wandering time is come.
—Eskimo song

The Eleusinian Mysteries

Some scholars say Procession Day was the true beginning of the Mysteries. On this day, the crowds and initiates walked the Sacred Road, the road from Athens to Eleusis. On the way, they performed rituals, made offerings, danced, and sang. Women may have dressed as Baubo and lifted their skirts as the Mystai passed by. According to Demetra George, "The Eleusinians, draped in sheets, began to mock and insult the initiates, even the most important officials, revealing secret and humiliating truths about each person, who had to listen to the abuse without being able to reply. Thus exposed, the old self…died for shame."[37]

The procession reached Eleusis and the sacred grounds of the temple by nightfall. At this time the exhausted and hungry Mystai probably proceeded inside.

The Salmon Mysteries

In our story, this is when Demeter walks and walks until she comes to a stone wall. She is so exhausted she cannot think. She is so tired she cannot see the path which is almost right in front of her. She asks Cougar for help. Cougar offers her a ride and carries her over the water to the other side and then up the waterfall to level ground.

Cougars are amazing members of our community here in the Pacific Northwest and throughout much of North America. The *felis concolor* probably has more common names than any other creature in our country: mountain lion, puma, cougar, panther, catamount to name just a few. The cougar "played an important role in the religious beliefs of the Pueblo Indians in New Mexico and Arizona."[38] Because of the cougar's great hunting skills, hunter societies often looked to the cougar as a magical hunting ally, wishing to take on the strength and skill of the cougar. The mountain lion was a protector and guardian to many of the Southwest people; to some the cat had the power to cure as well as to kill.[39]

The cougar was often Coyote's elder and wiser sibling. In our area, white pioneers wrote about panthers following their children to and from school. When I first heard this story, I assumed the cats were stalking the children, but apparently the children regarded them almost as pets—much to the distress of the parents who usually hunted the cat and killed it when they found out about the "cougar guardians." This has also happened in modern times. As a child, the writer Rod McKuen lived in Prindle, Washington, and he remembers a cougar following him to the bus stop. Like coyotes, cougars are often reviled by humans, and Wildlife Services are called in to dispatch many unfortunate cats.

In ancient Crete, lions were often shown protecting the Great Goddess. In some cultures, the lions became goddesses. The lion-headed Egyptian goddess Sekhmet became so disgusted with humans that she began slaughtering them with the intent of wiping them out completely. The gods weren't happy with this particular turn of events, so they got Sekhmet drunk. When she woke up from her drunken stupor, her rage was spent.

Bast, a kinder gentler cat goddess, was also worshipped throughout Egypt. Barbara Walker notes: "The Greeks identified Bast with Artemis, whose Roman name was Diana,…widely known…as the Queen of Witches. Therefore the cat was identified with witchcraft and…Goddess worship."[40] The cougar is similarly linked with the goddess in our story.

Mystai Tasks

Today you might want to make your own procession. Take a hike in the woods with friends or create a dance procession around your own house. While I don't think taunting each other with insults is a good idea, telling jokes and having a good belly laugh is always appropriate. Women (and men) already carry around so much shame; we don't want our former selves to "die of shame." But we can look at what we don't want to carry around any more and use these Mysteries as an opportunity to set our burdens down. Think of the transformative journey of the salmon. The salmon swim from fresh water to salt water back to fresh water, and they change physically to accommodate those environments.

What caused your belly laugh today?

Before you go to sleep tonight, remember the strength of Demeter and the Cougar who carried her across the river. Even the strongest of us need help on our journeys. Blessed be!

Write about your day today.

_____

_____

_____

_____

_____

_____

_____

_____

_____

_____

_____

_____

Record dreams here.

Day Seven: Day of the Bear

You who seek to know Me, know that your seeking and yearning will avail you not, unless you know the Mystery: for if that which you seek, you find not within yourself, you will never find it without.
—Doreen Valiente, adapted by Starhawk

The Eleusinian Mysteries

According to Mara Lynn Keller, September 20th was "a final day of preparation, of resting, purification, fasting and sacrifice. To sacrifice, literally 'to make holy,' meant giving up, offering over to the Goddess whatever was hindering the soul's journey along its path."[41]

The Salmon Mysteries

In The Salmon Mysteries, Demeter walks and walks and walks, without eating or sleeping. Her grief and rage drop away. She can go on no longer. She asks Bear for help. Bear tells her she must eat, sleep, and drink. Demeter doesn't have time for such things, she says. Bear insists. So Demeter eats, sleeps, and drinks. After she is rested, after she is fully embodied, she has a dream and realizes the map is in her body. *She knows the way.*

Nowadays, it seems everyone is "too busy." We give up time with family and friends to work, work, work. We over-schedule ourselves and our children so that we go, go, go. We say we don't have time to meditate, exercise, take a hike, or sit and do nothing. No time, no time, no time.

At the end of our lives are we going to want to remember all the times we spent in the car shuffling people back and forth? Do we want to remember how many hours we spent at work? Is working too hard and running back and forth easier than having quality time with our family and friends?

As a culture we are relationship-starved. We are so stressed that the idea of making friends and nurturing those friendships seems like too much work: Everyone gets on your nerves anyway, don't they? Being on the go and working too hard is certainly easier than sitting with ourselves quietly and discovering the hard truths about our lives.

Yet if we neglect ourselves, we get sick or become impatient, irritable, and exhausted. Wouldn't it be better for everyone if we did take the time to *nourish* ourselves? Just as Demeter did. Once she takes care of herself, she is able to sleep and dream. She gets in touch with her true inner self: *the Goddess who knows*.

Not only does Demeter rest at this point, she lets go of her grief and rage. She has felt it. She has not ignored it. She has acted upon it by looking for her daughter, but now she lets it go. Her exhaustion acts as a catalyst for this sacrifice—this letting go. Then she is able to comply with Bear's request that she take care of herself. She is ready for the next part of her journey.

Humans have revered the bear for as long as we have been on this planet. "Neanderthals of 100,000 years ago placed skulls of the giant cave bear in a shrinelike manner near their dwellings,"[42] Laura C. Martin says. Indigenous people in North America and Siberia believed the bear was a shapeshifter and humans were descendants of the bear. Siberian hunters employed elaborate hunting rituals when going after the bear to protect themselves and the bear.

The bear, the biggest mammal in North America, is often associated with the goddess—and with women. The bear is a symbol of strength, protection, and healing. She is a fierce mother who will go after anyone who gets in the way of her and her cubs. She knows when and what to eat and how and when to rest and take care of herself. She stores food in her body for the long winter and understands the value of sleep and dreaming.

Nordic followers of the Goddess Ursel donned bear-skins which transformed them into fierce warriors: berserkers. Buffie Johnson says "the bear inspires awe and fascination, embodying as it does the spirit of the wild and of the Goddess as Mother....Celts venerated Dea Artia, a bear goddess. The name of the Celtic Fire Goddess, Bridgit, stems from the word for bear."[43] Artemis, goddess of the wild, was called the Bear Goddess. Bears were often powerful allies for shamans and other healers.

Demeter listens to Bear. She rests her head in the lap of the wild and dreams the wild dream. Demeter has crossed over into the world of the wild, but it is not the wild caused by uncontrolled grief. She is no longer Bigfoot or a representative of life out of balance. She is inhabiting her authentic wild Nature. It is in this wild state, with the wild, that she will find answers. And so she sleeps.

Demeter also eats. It is necessary before she can step over the threshold and see her daughter again. Once she eats the berries, she is able to truly see.

Plants make up more than 99% of the living matter on this planet. What is more amazing and miraculous than a plant? From a tiny seed grows a mighty oak or a beautiful flower or a vine that produces seemingly endless amounts of zucchinis. Plants are able to convert light into food to create their own tissue. We can't do that. We need to first eat plants and then our bodies can build new cells. Without plants, we wouldn't exist. Yet most people go through their days without acknowledging or even noticing the very beings which provide them with air and food. Many people walk around lonely and relationship-starved while all around them living beings—plants—are reaching out, reaching down, whispering, shouting, feeding, revealing, nourishing and sharing.

Once Demeter slows down and consciously eats, she is prepared to be reunited: She is ready to be whole again.

Mystai Tasks

For you on this seventh day, be conscious of what you eat and drink. Write about it you wish, or draw your day. But also feel free just to beee. Rest and dream. (Blank pages at the end of the chapter.)

_____

_____

_____

_____

_____

Record dreams here.

Day Eight: Mysteriotides Nychtes, Night of the Mysteries

The beauty of the Way is that there is no "way."
—Loy Ching-Yuen, The Book of the Heart

The Eleusinian Mysteries

No one alive really knows what went on inside the temple during the two nights of the Mysteries. During the week leading up to the Night of the Mysteries initiates may (or may not) have fasted, so they may have been exhausted upon reaching the sacred grounds of the temple. At that point they may have drunk *kykeon* (herb-flavored barley-water which may or may not have been an intoxicant) as they went into the Telesterion.

Once inside, the initiates (and others who had experienced the Mysteries before) may have witnessed a reenactment of the Demeter and Persephone myth, although many scholars vehemently argue against this scenario. The initiates may or may not have been in the dark. They may have seen and heard frightening things and then had the Goddess revealed to them. They may or may not have been forced, somehow, to face their fear of death.

Some time during the Mysteries, the initiates may have reached into the sacred baskets and held the sacred objects. Then they may have recited something like, "I have fasted, I have drunk the *kykeon*, and I have taken things out of the basket and put them back."

On the second night of the Mysteries some kind of sacred marriage may have been reenacted. The Goddess may have given birth to the divine child.

More than a few historians and scholars believe that "the reveal" near the end of the Mysteries was a single stalk of grain—Demeter was, after all, the grain goddess to many.

But no one knows for certain what happened, and even if we did, it probably would not mean to us what it did to the Greeks and others who worshipped Demeter and Persephone. Initiation "into the Eleusinian Mysteries was a process," Patricia Monaghan writes. "The moment of initiation was just…a moment."[44] The Mysteries were about transformation—"transformation of the hearts of the initiates."[45]

The Salmon Mysteries

In our story, we now follow Persephone. She returns from the Ocean to the Land of the Salmon people. The Salmon People welcome Persephone to her new home. She does not want to stay, but they don't want to let her go. Interestingly, she does not try to escape. Instead, she sits by the water. She, too, must grieve her loss—the loss of who she *was*.

It could be argued that Persephone's journey into the Underworld is precipitated by menarche. She starts out golden and ends up bloody red. Menarche marks the beginning of enormous change in a girl's life, one most of us don't really comprehend at the time it is actually happening. Our bodies are transforming—transmutating, really—in so many ways. We are manufacturing new chemicals and hormones and pumping them into our bloodstream. We are like the salmon changing from fresh water to ocean water.

Ancient people considered women's menstrual blood as a powerful magical fluid. Bleeding women were magical, better able to access their wisdom at this time, and potentially dangerous if they didn't have their blood power under control. A girl's first blood was especially valued and was often used on fields to ensure their productivity.

This deepening which happens during menstruation parallels Persephone's journey into the Underworld. In a way, she has no control over what is happening. She falls into the river. We're born women, so we bleed monthly. Persephone could see her journey to the Underworld as a terrible accident and burden, or she can go with the flow of it, so to speak, and access those subtle (and sometimes not so subtle) energies which become available during bleeding times (and journeys to the Underworld).

Once a woman begins to bleed, everything changes in her life. She is no longer a girl: She is a young woman. She can sit along the sidelines mourning her loss, as Persephone does for a time, or she can learn from her journey and step into her power and womanhood.

Persephone's journey could also illustrate what a menopausal woman experiences. Coming to the end of menstruation can be equally as confusing and taxing as adolescence! Persephone begins the story as a young woman. Perhaps she falls into the river during menarche. She lives her life in the Ocean. Then as she gets near menopause—when soon the wise blood fills her and she is red with its power—she returns home. We leave our mothers as young women, experience our lives, then often return when we are older. Menopause is its own powerful journey to the Underworld.

For our purposes today, let's keep Persephone as a relatively young woman. She comes to this new village. She does not participate in the community; she doesn't eat or sleep. Finally, a group of young women sit with her. They probably tell jokes, the way young girls do, and giggle and lean against one another. They begin to do things together, and Persephone learns the ways of the tribe. This is very reminiscent of what happens to young girls in "real life." When they become teenagers they are awkward and often don't know how to behave. They don't want to be around their mothers, yet they don't want to be away from them. Usually they find a core group of girls which become—for good or ill—the center of their lives for a time. From them, they learn the ways of the tribe.

In our own lives, we fall into the Underworld for a variety of reasons: illness, grief, loss, mid-life, menstruation, menopause. Sometimes it is an awful journey, filled with peril and horror, where everything seems absolutely out of our control. Other times we are able to relax and see these journeys as times of deepening and transformation.

Eventually boys fight for Persephone's attention. One's hands had to be blood-free to participate in the Mysteries—no killers allowed. This is a rather remarkable requirement given the nature of the patriarchy. (Although the caveat was no one with "unexpiated" blood on their hands could participate.) Persephone won't have anything to do with these warriors and is instead attracted to a peaceful young man who sits next to her and points out the stars to her.

Persephone soon becomes proficient in the ways of the Salmon People. She is a great comfort to these people whose numbers are diminishing and who feel like no one pays them any heed. She chooses her own name: Persephone. In this land, this Underworld, this Otherworld, Persephone learns to use fire. In fact, she learns to *Dance with Fire*. She becomes the best of all of those who can dance with fire.

Then one day Persephone looks over and sees her mother, the goddess Demeter; Demeter has just eaten the protective huckleberries and stepped over the threshold. Thresholds were numinous places. Before grain could be turned into bread, it had to be threshed and winnowed. Threshing consisted of pounding the grain with a flail. This released the grain from the straw. The threshold was a board on the floor which kept the precious grain from falling through the cracks. According to Pauline Campanelli, these threshing floors were considered so sacred that "when King David entered Judea, he purchased a threshing floor upon which he built a temple. The threshing floor had such a powerful link to fertility that even today…the groom must carry the bride across the threshold on their wedding night."[46]

The threshing room was a place of transition. The wheat went into the room as a plant and came out as a grain and straw. The grain could then be cooked or milled into flour for bread. How appropriate for the Grain Goddess to step over a threshold to find Her Daughter who has just gained the knowledge of fire and can now convert her Mother's bounty—threshed grain—into food.

Huckleberries were a staple food of Pacific Northwest Native Americans, and no fall feast was complete without them. Even now in the late summer and early fall, area residents go out huckleberry picking. Huckleberries bestowed protection and magical dreams on those who ate them.[47]

Demeter now sees her daughter as a powerful young woman, a goddess in her own right. They embrace. Demeter gives Persephone the huckleberries: the wild food; Persephone gives Demeter the bread: the cooked food.

Demeter wants her daughter back. At first, Persephone isn't certain what she wants to do. Demeter is prepared to offer the Salmon People something very valuable: She as the goddess will teach their ways to the rest of the world. She will teach humans to keep the air and waters clean, and she will teach the rituals and songs the humans need to know so that the salmon will keep coming back to the river. This is a tremendously valuable gift. She is essentially giving life to those in the Underworld—to those who are already dead. *She is giving life back to that which was extinct.*

Demeter offers to do what is absolutely necessary for our planet. The Earth has taken care of us forever. Yet just as Demeter wanted her beloved daughter by her side, the Earth needs love and attention. She cannot feed us if we continue to destroy the environment as we are doing. It is all connected. We are all connected. Demeter loses her daughter and doesn't get her back immediately because the Salmon People need her. They need to keep Persephone because there aren't enough Salmon People left. The landscape withers and dies because Demeter does not have the love of her life, and she doesn't have the love of her life because the landscape has withered and died previously, metaphorically, because of the degradation of the environment.

Persephone learns to use and control fire while in the Underworld. By being able to control fire, Persephone becomes a shaman, channelling energy in many ways: for healing, transformation, rebirth, sustenance. She learns to cook. Menarche opened the door to her sexuality. She learns to "cook" her passion as well as her food.

Persephone becomes a true magician because of her journey to the Underworld. In Vicki Noble's *Motherpeace: A Way to the Goddess Through Myth, Art and Tarot*, she titles the chapter on the tarot card Magician "Dancing the Fire." She writes, "The alchemy of fire is the Magician's great secret. Her activating power changes one thing into another. Of all early techniques, fire was the most powerful and versatile: it allowed people to turn grain into bread, clay into stone, inflammable matter to ashes…The original power of the female group to harness and use fire is acknowledged in mythology all over the world and pertains to the sexual fire as well as the use of physical fire for cooking and transformation mysteries.…The shaman channels healing heat—the fire of the universe coming through the human being."[48]

Imagine all of your life that you are surrounded by this beautiful golden plant. Then one day, someone teaches you how you can survive by eating this formerly inedible plant. Fire transforms the grain into bread. You mill it, you shape it, you add water and maybe some leavening to it, but essentially, it is the fire that transmutes this grain into food.

This would be a miracle.

Archaeologists have found miniature knives with grass resins on them in caves in France. This indicates our Neolithic ancestors harvested wild grains. Vicki Noble tells us that "scholars found the charred remains of fire, mortars and pestles for grinding grains, and the remains of bread having been baked in the primitive ovens. All this took place near ritual cave sanctuaries…later in Çatal Hüyük, the bread would be baked in the courtyard ovens of the ritual temples where priestesses led the sacred ceremonies."[49]

Demeter provides the plants; Persephone provides the means to convert these plants into food. Persephone enables us to access the nutrients of the Goddess's plants. By teaching us to cook, essentially, Persephone becomes the true link between people and the Goddess—people and the Earth. She is what we need to reestablish our connection with Nature: fire and the ability to use it peacefully. We don't build weapons with it, we don't create nuclear bombs with it. *We cook with it. We cook our sexuality. We cook the gifts of the Earth.*

Mystai Tasks

For you today, try and attend the Day of Mystery with a group of people. (In the next chapter I outline one possible scenario for the Day of Mystery.) But if that doesn't work for you, create it just for you. I've done the Mysteries solo many years. Dress in your Mystai clothes.

If you are meeting with others, bring your workbook if there's anything you wish to share. Bring along your sacred objects, blank poster board and pictures, guidebook, journal, and lunch. If you're doing this with a group, it's also respectful to bring the Priestess or whoever is hosting the Mysteries a gift. This isn't something you need to buy, just something which conveys your respect and appreciation. If you are acting as initiate and priestess, remember to gift yourself.

Journal any of your plans here.

_____

_____

_____

_____

_____

_____

_____

_____

_____

_____

_____

_____

_____

_____

Record dreams here.

The Day of Mystery

Thrice happy are those who have seen the Mysteries.
—Sophocles (496-408 B.C.E.)

What was the mystery? On this day more than any, you and your communities are the creatrices and creators. Below, I will relate one of the ways you can celebrate the Day of Mystery with a group. You can also adapt this for solitary use. If you want to duplicate this ceremony, the woman acting as Melissa should first read this chapter all the way through.

But please feel free to plan your own "mystery." It's about going through the process, getting to know thyself, beginning to understand the mystery of life, and acknowledging your passage from initiate to priestess, from Mystai to Melissa. My own "mystery" event or celebration gets simpler and simpler with each year.

So this is how we've done it in my community as a group, but I've also done it solo.

You'll need to designate a place as a Goddess Temple for this Day of Mystery. Set aside two rooms and decorate appropriately. One place is where you will all celebrate together. This is normally indoors so that the Priestess/Melissa can contain the energy. Think of this as the Outer Chamber. This could be something the Melissa decorates alone or you could do it as a group.

Have clay in the Outer Chamber that will be used later. Each Mystes will use this in an exercise I detail below.

The Melissa creates the Inner Chamber alone. This is where each Mystes will go to be by herself. Make this place beautiful and dark and mysterious. I tend to make my Inner Chambers cave-like, cramped. I decorate it with lots of beautiful goddess and nature pictures, but I leave it dark, so the Mystes can't see these until her meditation is over. I put an extension cord with a light switch on it so when the Mystes is finished with her meditation she can turn on the light. (More details below.) Put an urn or some kind of container near where the Mystai will be.

Mystes: Remember to bring your *hiera* and dress in your Mystes garments.

Upon entering the house—the Goddess Temple as the Mystes—place your folded hands at your heart center. This helps open your heart. The Melissa (Demeter's Priestess) will ask you (or you can ask yourself):

Have you come prepared? Yes.

Have you walked the Sacred Way? Yes.

Have you dreamed along the Sacred Way? Yes.

Have you danced along the Sacred Way? Yes.

Have you eaten along the Sacred Way? Yes.

Then you come prepared. Welcome, Daughter.

(The Melissa may make the sign of the star on your forehead, throat, and heart with essence of amber or another essential oil diluted with vegetable oil. Or you can do it yourself. If you don't like the star, pick another symbol that represents this process for you.)

Melissa: *We gather together today to receive the blessings of the Goddess. Bless us in our endeavors, Goddess Mother.*

Mystai response: *Bless us, Goddess Mother.*

The Melissa may then lead the Mystai in a grounding exercise followed by chanting and/or an Invocation to the Ancestors.

Invocation to the Ancestors

O my Ancestors
Upon your ashes I walk through life
Upon your dust I shall one day rest

O my Ancestors
You who flew above the Earth
You who burned with Passion
You who made your home in the Ocean
You who burrowed deep into the Earth

O my Ancestors
I ask for your blessings
And thank you for my life

Ashes to ashes
Dust to dust
All my relations
O my Ancestors

The Dance

After this, you may want to dance as a group. Put on "The Calling" from Santana's *Supernatural* album. Or some of Hildegard of Bingen's music. Something which makes you move. Dance the Snake. Find direction through your body. Then Dance the Salmon. In the river, out in the ocean, up the river again. Imagine the rivers filled with wild salmon again.

Afterward have some refreshments, sit and relax for a bit.

Going Deep

At this point, the Melissa may read aloud the following meditation (or something like it) as the Mystai sit with a piece of the clay nearby:

"You have come the Sacred Way. You have begun the transformation. You have danced the Snake Dance. Now you are ready to let go of that which weighs you down, that which keeps you from becoming your true self.

"Meditate on your process during the last week. Then contemplate your life. Think of incidents in your life which bring you grief and pain. Ask yourself if you are ready to let them go. If you are, take a small piece of clay. Roll it into a tiny ball. As you shape it between your hands, think about what you are ready to release. Let the energy of this flow into the ball. You are letting go of it. Letting go. It is now in the ball of clay, safe, with harm to none. Is there something else you wish to release? A bad habit? A bad memory? Let it go into another ball of clay, turn it over to Mother Earth. Release it."

When you as the Mystes have completed this task, take your clay balls and go into the Inner Chamber. (One Mystes at a time.) Here in this dark place, crawl into the cramped cave. Sit in this darkness. Meditate on releasing all that is harmful to you. You may grow uncomfortable in the confined space. The time will seem to go on and on. When you are ready, when you believe you are truly prepared to release your burdens, dump the clay balls into the urn the Melissa left in the Inner Chamber. Your burdens are now released.

You might say, "Thank you, Mother Earth Goddess, for taking my burdens. May they cause harm to none."

Now make a promise to do something for your community over the next year. It doesn't have to be huge. You don't have to promise to save the salmon from extinction, but you could promise to volunteer at one of the local environmental or peace groups. You could start a recycling drive in your neighborhood, or you could start recycling in your own house. You decide.

When you've made your promise out loud, turn on the light.

Watch the world transform! The light chases away most of the dark but not all, and you can see what was in the dark all along: the Goddess. Pictures and statues of Her adorn the cave and the room. Flowers are strewn everywhere. It is a beautiful living shrine to the Goddess.

When you are finished, turn off the light again and leave the cave. Once you have returned to the Outer Temple and the other Mystai, begin a collage documenting your experience of the Mysteries. Do this in silence, with music on in the background.

The urn of "baggage balls" can be later taken out to the river—as long as you have used clean river clay without additional ingredients—or it may be ceremonially buried, either as part of the day or as a task the Priestess will perform later.

Breaking Bread Together:

At this point, eat something together: slices from the same apple, pieces from the same bread (gluten-free if need be to make it safe for everyone). (We used to make bread during these ceremonies, but it became too task-oriented and people got tired. Now we usually eat an apple together.)

After they have eaten some, the Melissa can say:

Demeter, Persephone, you have shown us the key.
Bless these women, they are all your kin.
The Mysteries are done and have just begun.
Mystes once, Melissa today.
We have found the Sacred Way!
Blessed beeee!
The Circle is open but unbroken.
Merry meet and merry part and merry meet again.

As the group finishes eating, you can share any thoughts or feelings. Then help clean up and prepare for the Sacred Feast!

Mystai Tasks

Write about your day.

Kim Antieau

Any last notes about the feast?

Record your dreams.

Draw your day.

Day Nine: Day of the Salmon

And the Great Mother said:
Come my child and give me all that you are…
You are not alone and you have never been alone….
—Linda Reuther, from *Homecoming*

Eleusinian Mysteries

The Mysteries and celebration are now winding down, and the people offer libations to their ancestors and the Goddess.

The Salmon Mysteries

Demeter and Persephone feast with the Salmon People, then return home to teach others the sacred salmon ways.

Mystai Tasks

After any initiation, transformation, or pilgrimage, we must go back to our communities and families. To our lives. At first everything seems the same as it was before the Mysteries began. Nothing has miraculously changed. You may still feel burdened. This is only a habit. Remind yourself again and again that you have been released from your burdens, and act as if it is so. This doesn't mean suppressing your emotions. It means the Mysteries are a beginning. Now you need to learn to stay out of your ruts permanently. You may have to jump out of them again and again. But you can do it! Life is a process, and so are the Mysteries.

Part of your responsibility now is to step back into the community and bring your wisdom, your whole True Self, with you. The Day of the Salmon is a good way to begin.

You could invite your community (or at least part of it) to share in an Autumnal Equinox Feast. Many of our ancestors considered Fall Equinox to be the Second Harvest, or Thanksgiving. Equinox was a time of balance, when the world hung on the edge of the light for a moment before moving toward the dark. Where I live, in the Columbia River Gorge, this is when we pick berries and welcome the salmon back home.

Our ancestors gathered together often to celebrate the bounty of the Earth. They followed particular rituals or customs. In some places, the bones of the first salmon—unburnt—were thrown back into the river. The last sheaf of grain to be harvested was dressed up as the Goddess and put at the head of the table. Food was prepared with care, with the knowledge that it was a gift from the Earth. By cooking and eating food in a sacred manner, our ancestors were honoring the Earth and guaranteeing future bounty. They knew where all their food had come from. They had faith that the hunters, gatherers, and fishers took their harvest in a sacred way. Food was their direct connection to the Earth, Nature, and one another.

Each food at a feast held a particular significance. For example, they believed garlic and onion bestowed protection on the user. (They were right; both help us guard against colds and other illnesses.) According to Scott Cunningham, "Garlic was eaten on festival days to Hecate, and was left at a crossroads as a sacrifice in her name."[50] Bread, the staff of life, was added to the table in honor of Demeter. Olives or an olive branch honored Athena and symbolized peace. Cinnamon drew money and good health to the lucky user; peppermint brought love and stimulation.[51] Women ate eggs, the perennial symbols of fertility, to help them conceive. Eggs were a central part in curing ceremonies all over the world. In indigenous medicine today, the use of eggs to help draw the disease out of a person is still prevalent. The egg—the disease now safely contained within—is then ceremoniously buried.

Today, most people walking in a vegetable garden or out in the woods could not identify which plants were which, let alone know the medicinal or magical properties for each plant. Most people who buy fish and meat have no idea in what manner the animals were raised, treated, and slaughtered. Girls and women (and increasingly boys and men) suffer from exploding rates of anorexia, bulimia, and other food disorders. More and more people are developing food sensitivities. We have lost our connection to food and therefore have lost our living, healing connection with the Earth.

"For a long time now, we have been unable to remember our former closeness with the Earth," Paul Devereux, John Steele, and David Kubrin write in *Earthmind*. "Due to this amnesia, the ecological problems now thrust upon us have come as a shock....We notice the emergence of an amnesia that is really a double forgetting, wherein a culture forgets, and then forgets that it has forgotten how to live in harmony with the planet."[52]

Some believe it is too late to reestablish our connection to the planet; we may have had an intuitive relationship with Nature at one time, but it has long since been bred out of us. Besides, isn't the biosphere dying anyway and there's nothing we can do about it? Others maintain that everything is fine, we shouldn't think about negative things, and it'll all go away.

We ignore the state of the biosphere at our peril. Whether we are connected to our food and environment or not, we eat, we breathe, we consume, and our bodies tell us exactly how the planet is doing. Humans are experiencing epidemic rates of cancer and immune dysfunction illnesses.

We need help, and the Earth needs our help. In Sarah A. Conn's essay "When the Earth Hurts, Who Responds?" she encourages us to "actively seek out a connection with the natural world that will sustain" us and the world and to (1) become aware of the larger world, (2) cultivate an emotional responsiveness to the world (3) develop and understand the interconnectedness of global problems, and (4) take action on behalf of the Earth.[53]

One of the ways to take action is to reestablish our link, individually and collectively, to our food. Practical ways to do this are: (1) Buy whole foods without preservatives and chemicals. (2) Seasonally buy organic food from local farmers (organic factory farms can cause harm, too, just as commercial factory farms do). (3) Don't use chemical pesticides and fertilizers. The use of pesticides and chemical fertilizers has caused more environmental (and human) damage than almost anything else we're doing. (4) Grow your own organic garden. Nothing quite gets you in touch with the Earth as digging around in the dirt does!

If you eat meat, eat organic. It's better for you and the animals. Same goes with eggs and cheeses. If you eat fish, find out which ones are safe (for your health and the environment).

This brings us to our sacred salmon, the lifeblood and soul of the Pacific Northwest. Wild salmon are in trouble. If you eat salmon, it's best to ask for and buy wild salmon. Farmed salmon pollute. They are raised in floating pens and produce a great deal of waste which ruins local marine environments; this waste can spread disease and it is full of the antibiotics the fish are given, which then can be harmful to humans and cause problems along shorelines. Farmed salmon can escape. Since the farmed salmon here in the Pacific are actually Atlantic salmon, it becomes an exotic species when it escapes and can contaminate already precarious native stocks. Wild salmon is better for you; it has higher levels of the Omega-3 fatty acids. Farmed salmon is injected with dye to give it the pink color wild salmon get from the wild food they eat.

Some wild salmon runs are still thriving. Buy fish that have been caught from those areas. If a store sells wild salmon, they know where they get it from. For instance, if you buy salmon from the Columbia River you should know that the river has high levels of dioxin; plus radioactive waste from Hanford is continually leaking into it. However, you could consider how long the salmon actually spend in the river compared with how long they are in the ocean—and that actually depends upon whether it is a wild salmon or a hatchery salmon. The hatchery salmon tend to stay closer to "home" and spend less time in the ocean than the wild salmon.

It is a complex issue. Food and sustenance should be simpler than this. And it can be. Try buying locally, seasonally, organically. See if that helps with your relationship with food and Nature.

One of the other ways we can work on our connection to the world is by participating in communal celebrations. Coming together to honor the turning of the Wheel of the Year—and to celebrate the return of the Salmon, for example—helps establish connections with each other and the rest of the planet. We express our gratitude for our plenty, we thank the Visibles and the Invisibles, and we eat together. We eat the same food, essentially, and are linked by it: It is a supremely intimate act. Celebrating in this way becomes a communal prayer to the forces of Nature, to the Divine.

Part of your duty now as a Melissa, as one who has been initiated into the Mysteries, is to participate fully in this celebratory feast by helping to cook the meal, bless the food and space, decorate, and make certain the guests are comfortable. (And help clean up after the festivities are over.)

Before eating, one of the Melissa, the hostess, or someone else should say a grace. The word grace means "to praise out loud." Saying grace hearkens back to our ancestors, some who prayed to the Graces. These Triple Goddesses were often depicted naked, attending Aphrodite. Their other name was Charites. They were probably very ancient goddesses. "The charis or 'grace' they bestowed was the gift of the Goddess: beauty, kindness, love, tenderness, pleasure, creativity, artistry, and sensuality."[54] To say grace out loud, then, is to call upon the Graces to bring love and joy to your table. What a wonderful gift for your guests!

With this feast, on the final day of the Mysteries, we celebrate the wondrous mystical journey of the salmon and the reuniting of Demeter and Persephone. We celebrate the momentary balance of light and dark. We begin weaving the threads back into the tapestry of life. This is a great and wonderful task. Thank you for being a part of it.

Write about the day, including the food you chose and what it meant.

Record dreams here.

___

Can you hear Demeter whisper? You are the weaver, the tiller, the seed, the fruit, the bread, the oven, the fire. You are the child and the mother. The water and the salmon. The phoenix and the crow. The coyote and the belly laugh. The Milky Way and the stars. You are the heart and the heartbeat.

You are embraced. Held. Even in those times when you cannot get your face out of the muddy splash of memory or despair or sickness. Wait. Breathe. Wait. Breathe. I am there in the pause. And there again. I am your heart and your breath and the slap of your soles against my Earthy soul. Down and dirty. I await you. Sister, Daughter, Son, Mother, Grandmother. Blessings.

In your dream you met Demeter
Splendid and severe, who said: Endure...
Peace daughter. Find your true kin.
      —then you felt her kiss.
         —Genevieve Taggard, from "Demeter"

Song of the Salmon

I celebrate myself and sing myself,
And what I assume you shall assume,
For every atom belongs to me as good belongs to you.
—Walt Whitman, from *Song of Myself*

I sing the song of myself
As I wiggle from my mother's sac
Resting here on the floor of my world.
Is it your world, too?

The gravel tickles my belly.
The water washes all around me.
I laugh and am filled with myself,
With this river, this world.

I eat the bones of my ancestors.
All the delicacies (and indelicacies)
Of this place I call home.
Is it your home, too?

What is above my wavering sky?
What is below this sandy bottom?
The water embraces me!
I ride the currents. Ahhh bliss!

This is the Big River I now travel,
Isn't it? I have heard the stories!
The water changes me. My body longs for—
What? What do I long for?

Ocean! Depths I cannot imagine!
Bodies bumping against my body.
I dance, dance, dance.
Move. What is this feeling?

This new longing. I have seen.
I have felt. I have experienced.
Mother, these depths make me ache
For home. I am changing

Shapeshifting. Bloody red
I pulse with desire. Creativity
Explodes. In my Being. Do
You feel this Ecstasy! This desire!

Home. Ahhh Bliss! Release.
Momma. I grow weary. Time
To step out of this Bloody Dress.
Soon I will be fish food.

Other bodies knock against
Me. Bedraggled. Bedecked.
I await the nibbles of my
Children. As they eat of my body.

I sing the song of myself.
Of life in this glorious body
Tied to this Earthy place.
Is it your body too?

—Kim Antieau
Stevenson, Washington
September 2002

Any last thoughts or art until next year.

Notes

1. Vicki Noble, *Motherpeace: a way to the goddess through myth, art, and tarot* (New York: HarperCollins: 1994), 101.

2. Norma Lorre Goodrich, *Priestess* (New York: HarperCollins, 1989), 3.

3. Mara Lynn Keller, "The Eleusinian Mysteries of Demeter and Persephone: Fertility, Sexuality, and Rebirth," *Journal of Feminist Studies in Religion* v. 4, no. 1, (1988,) 33.

4. Kathie Carlson, *Life's Daughter/Death's Bride: Inner Transformations Through the Goddess Demeter/Persephone*, (Boston: Shambhala, 1997), p.39.

5. Keller, 28.

6. Keller, 27.

7. Carl Kerényi, *Eleusis: Archetypal Image of Mother and Daughter*, tr. Ralph Manheim (New York: Schocken Books, 1977), 15.

8. Keller, 28.

9. Jane Corddry Langill, "Kamuy Yukar: Song of the Wife of Okikurmi," in *First Fish, First People: Salmon Tales of the North Pacific*, ed. Judith Roche and Meg McHutchison, (Seattle: University of Washington Press, 1998), 29.

10. Elizabeth Woody, "Twanat, to follow behind the ancestors," in *First Fish* (see note 9), 76.

11. Ibid, 76.

12. Ibid, 76-78.

13. Mara Freeman, *Kindling the Celtic Spirit* (New York: HarperCollins, 2001), 97.

14. Judith Roche and Meg McHutchison, editors, *First Fish* (see note 9).

15. Kerényi, 11.

16. Patricia Monaghan, *The New Book of Goddesses and Heroines* (St. Paul: Llewellyn, 1997), 60.

17. Barbara Walker, *The Woman's Encyclopedia of Myths and Secrets* (Edison, New Jersey: Castle Books, 1996) 213.

18. Merlin Stone, *Ancient Mirrors of Womanhood: A Treasury of Goddess and Heroine Lore from Around the World* (Boston: Beacon Press, 1991), 369.

19. Layne Redmond, *When the Drummers were Women: A Spiritual History of Rhythm* (New York: Three Rivers Press, 1997), 128.

20. Carolyn McVickar Edwards, *The Storyteller's Goddess: Tales of the Goddess and her Wisdom from Around the World* (San Francisco: HarperCollins, 1991), 178.

21. Keller, 49.

22. Elinor W. Gadon, *The Once and Future Goddess* (San Francisco: Harper & Row, 1989), 143.

23. Zsuzsanna E. Budapest, *The Grandmother of Time: a woman's book of celebrations, spells, and sacred objects for every month of the year* (San Francisco: Harper & Row, 1989), 182.

24. Gadon, 155.

25. Demetra George, *Mysteries of the Dark Moon: the Healing Power of the Dark Goddess* (New York: HarperCollins, 1992), 246.

26. Keller, 28.

27. Jean Chevalier and Alain Gheerbrant, *Dictionary of Symbols* (London: Penguin, 1996), 789.

28. Patricia Monaghan, *The Goddess Path* (St. Paul, Minnesota: Llewellyn, 1999), 140.

29. Robert Michael Pyle, *Where Bigfoot Walks: Crossing the Dark Divide* (Boston: Houghton Mifflin, 1995), 132.

30. Ibid, 133.

31. Ibid, 144.

32. Clarissa Pinkola Estés, *Women Who Run with the Wolves* (New York: Ballantine, 1992) 338.

33. Demetra George, handouts from a workshop on Healing Goddesses co-taught with Vicki Noble, March, 1997.

34. Buffie Johnson, *Lady of the Beasts: Ancient Images of the Goddess and Her Sacred Animals* (New York: HarperCollins, 1988) 133-161.

35. Vicki Noble, "Publisher's Letter," *Snake Power*, October 1989, 3.

36. Vicki Noble, *Shakti Woman: Feeling our fire, healing our world: the new female shamanism* (New York: HarperCollins, 1991), 111.

37. George, 244.

38. James H. Gunnerson, "Mountain lions and Pueblo Shrines in the American Southwest," in *Icons of Power: Feline Symbolism in the Americas*, (New York: Routledge, 1998), ed. Nicholas J. Saunders, 228.

39. Ibid, 234-235.

40. Barbara G. Walker, *The Woman's Dictionary of Symbols and Sacred Objects*, (New York: Harper and Row, 1988), 367.

41. Keller, 52.

42. Laura C. Martin, *Wildlife Folklore* (Old Saybrook, Connecticut: Globe Pequot Press, 1994), 11.

43. Johnson, 344.

44. Monaghan, *The Goddess Path*, 143.

45. Ibid.

46. Pauline Campanelli, *Ancient Ways: Reclaimineg Pagan Traditions* (St.

Paul, Minnesota: Llewellyn: 1992), 131.

47. Scott Cunningham, *Cunningham's Encyclopedia of Magical Herbs* (St. Paul, Minnesota: Llewellyn: 1990), 129.

48. Noble, *Motherpeace*, 29.

49. Noble, *Shakti Woman*, 24.

50. Cunningham, 109.

51. Ibid, 75-175.

52. Paul Devereux, et al, *Earthmind* (New York: Harper & Row, 1989), 2-3, quoted in *Ecopsychology: Restoring the Earth, Healing the Mind*, ed. Theodore Roszak, et al (San Francisco: Sierra Club Books, 1995), 61.

53. Sarah A. Conn, "When the Earth Hurts, Who Responds?" in *Ecopsychology: Restoring the Earth, Healing the Mind*, ed. Theodore Roszak, Mary E. Gomes, and Allen D. Kanner (San Francisco: Sierra Club Books, 1995), 166-171.

54. Walker, *Woman's Dictionary of Symbols and Sacred Objects*, 256.

Bibliography

Budapest, Zsuzsanna E. *The Grandmother of Time: a woman's book of celebrations, spells, and sacred objects for every month of the year*. San Francisco: Harper & Row, 1989.

Campanelli, Pauline. *Ancient Ways: Reclaiming Pagan Traditions*. St. Paul, Minnesota: Llewellyn, 1992.

Carlson, Kathie Carlson. *Life's Daughter/Death's Bride: Inner Transformations Through the Goddess Demeter/Persephone*. Boston: Shambhala, 1997.

Chevalier, Jean Chevalier and Alain Gheerbrant. *Dictionary of Symbols*. London: Penguin, 1996.

Conn, Sarah A. "When the Earth Hurts, Who Responds?" In *Ecopsychology: Restoring the Earth, Healing the Mind*. Ed. Theodore Roszak, et al. San Francisco: Sierra Club Books, 1995.

Cunningham, Scott. *Cunningham's Encyclopedia of Magical Herbs*. St. Paul, Minnesota: Llewellyn, 1990.

Devereux, Paul, et al. *Earthmind*. New York: Harper & Row, 1989 pp. 2-3, quoted in *Ecopsychology: Restoring the Earth, Healing the Mind*. Ed. Theodore Roszak, et al. San Francisco: Sierra Club Books, 1995.

Edwards, Carolyn McVickar. *The Storyteller's Goddess: Tales of the Goddess and her Wisdom from Around the World*. San Francisco: HarperCollins, 1991.

Estés, Clarissa Pinkola. *Women Who Run With the Wolves*. New York: Ballantine, 1992.

Freeman, Mara. *Kindling the Celtic Spirit*. New York: HarperCollins, 2001.

Gadon, Elinor W. *The Once and Future Goddess*. San Francisco: Harper & Row, 1989.

George, Demetra. *Mysteries of the Dark Moon: the Healing Power of the Dark Goddess*. New York: HarperCollins, 1992.

Goodrich, Norma Lorre. *Priestesses*. New York: HarperCollins, 1989.

Gunnerson, James H. "Mountain Lions and Pueblo Shrines in the American

Southwest." In *Icons of Power: Feline Symbolism in the Americas*. ed. Nicholas J. Saunders. New York: Routledge, 1998.

Keller, Mara Lynn."The Eleusinian Mysteries of Demeter and Persephone: Fertility, Sexuality, and Rebirth," *Journal of Feminist Studies in Religion* v. 4, no.1, 1988. pp. 27-54.

Kerényi, Carl. *Eleusis: Archetypal Image of Mother and Daughter*. Princeton, New Jersey: Princeton University Press, 1967.

Langill, Jane Corddry. Introduction to "Kamuy Yukar: Song of the Wife of Okikurmi." In *First Fish, First People: Salmon Tales of the North Pacific*. Ed. Judith Roche and Meg McHutchison. Seattle: University of Washington Press, 1998.

Martin, Laura C. *Wildlife Folklore*. Old Saybrook, Connecticut: Globe Pequot Press, 1994.

Monaghan, Patricia. *The Goddess Path*. St. Paul, Minnesota: Llewellyn, 1999.

Monaghan, Patricia. *The New Book of Goddesses and Heroines*. St. Paul: Llewellyn, 1997.

Noble, Vicki. *Motherpeace: a way to the goddess through myth, art, and tarot*. New York: HarperCollins, 1994.

Noble, Vicki. "Publisher's Letter." *Snake Power, Oct.* 1989.

Noble, Vicki. *Shakti Woman: Feeling our fire, healing our world: the new female shamanism*. New York: HarperCollins, 1991.

Pyle, Robert Michael. *Where Bigfoot Walks: Crossing the Dark Divide*. Boston: Houghton Mifflin, 1995.

Redmond, Layne. *When the Drummers were Women: a Spiritual History of Rhythm*. New York: Three Rivers Press, 1997.

Roche, Judith and Meg McHutchison, editors. *First Fish, First People: Salmon Tales of the North Pacific Rim*. Seattle: University of Washington Press, 1998.

Stone, Merlin. *Ancient Mirrors of Womanhood: A Treasury of Goddess and Heroine Lore from Around the World*. Boston: Beacon Press, 1991.

Walker, Barbara G. *The Woman's Dictionary of Symbols and Sacred Objects*. New York: Harper and Row, 1988.

Walker, Barbara. *The Woman's Encyclopedia of Myths and Secrets*. Edison, New Jersey: Castle Books, 1996.

Woody, Elizabeth. "Twanat, to follow behind the ancestors." In *First Fish, First People: Salmon Tales of the North Pacific*. Seattle: University of Washington Press, 1998.